REVOLUT
IN THE
21st CENT

Chris Harn

CW00525833

REVOLUTION IN THE 21st CENTURY

Chris Harman

Bookmarks Publications

About the author

Chris Harman is the author of *A People's History of the World* (Bookmarks 1998), *Economics of the Madhouse* (Bookmarks 1995) and *The Lost Revolution: Germany 1918 to 1923* (Bookmarks 1982). He is the editor of *International Socialism* and is a leading member of the Socialist Workers Party (www.swp.org.uk).

Revolution in the 21st century – Chris Harman

First published July 2007 by Bookmarks Publications,

c/o 1 Bloomsbury Street, London WC1B 3QE

© Bookmarks Publications

ISBN 9781905192250

Cover photograph Miners in La Paz, Bolivia, October 2003
    by Sebastian Hacher

Designed by Bookmarks Publications

Printed by Cambridge Printing

Contents

Introduction: Everything to fight for

THE FALL of the Berlin Wall and collapse of the decaying dictatorships of Eastern Europe and the Soviet Union in 1989-91 supposedly ended the struggle to replace capitalism with something better. Yet the first years of this century have seen a new spirit of resistance across the world.

It began just before the new century itself with the demonstrations around the World Trade Organisation meeting in Seattle in November 1999. The slogan "Another world is possible" resonated across continents, with ever larger and more militant protests in Prague, Melbourne, Dakar, Gothenburg and Genoa. The resistance then merged into the biggest movement against war the world has ever seen – tens of millions taking to the streets of major cities on 15 February 2003 – while in Latin America, popular uprisings overthrew governments from Argentina to Ecuador.

The resistance has grown deeper and drawn in wider numbers of people everywhere. In 2005 voters in France and the Netherlands threw established politics into turmoil by rejecting a European constitution that aimed to slash restraints on market forces. Later in the same year immigrant communities across France exploded in rage.

2006 saw French students leading millions of workers in successful protests against attempts to scrap the employment rights of young people, Venezuela's president Hugo Chavez declared his intention to implement "socialism for the 21st century", and an uprising toppled the government of Nepal. In Oaxaca, Mexico, a teachers' strike turned into a rebellion that drove the army and police from the city, while students in Chile and Greece followed the French example. By the time you read this, the resistance will have found fresh forms of expression and shaken the established order in new ways – and the numbers beginning to seek political answers outside those offered by the existing system will have grown.

At the beginning of the 1990s we were promised a "new world order" and told we had reached "the end of history". Capitalism was the only option for humanity, it was said, but there was no cause for worry because a "new economic paradigm" had banished economic crisis.

How quickly the illusions were shattered. For most people, even in more prosperous parts of the world, life has become more burdensome and less secure. An economic crisis at the beginning of the new century cost millions of jobs in the US, which an economic revival has not restored. Japan has suffered 12 years of economic stagnation, and the economies of continental Europe have proved incapable of denting an unemployment rate of 10 per cent. In the US, the richest society in history, 90 per cent of the population have seen no improvement in living standards in the past 30 years and half are worse off. This is despite an increase in the time spent at work by the average male worker in the US of 160 hours a year – equivalent to about one month. For women workers it is worse – on average they spend an additional 200 hours at work in a year. In Germany, the five million on the dole have had their benefits cut. In France, one-fifth of young people are jobless and others can find nothing more than insecure McJobs. In Britain, we face the longest working hours in Europe, yet more than half the children across swathes of London grow up in poverty.

Life in much of the rest of the world is incomparably worse. In sub-Saharan Africa average living standards have fallen steadily for 30 years. Hundreds of millions struggle each day to obtain the 2,000 calories a day required for life. There are periodic famines and tens of thousands of children die each day from malnutrition or diseases that have long been treatable – diarrhoea, dysentery, tuberculosis, malaria. In Latin America, poverty is not just the fate of millions in Nicaragua, Guatemala, Ecuador, Bolivia and Peru who have been poor for generations; it is the fate of tens of millions in the more economically advanced countries – Argentina, Mexico and Brazil.

Apologists for the system talk of the growth of China and India, omitting to mention that prosperity for the 10 or 20 per cent of people who make up the middle classes leaves hundreds of millions in desperate poverty in the countryside. Hence, 150 million Chinese migrate to the cities each year to traipse the streets as casual labourers, and an epidemic of suicide convulses communities of indebted farmers in the more "prosperous" states of India.

Poverty is not the only nightmare for a huge section of the world's people. Many suffer the barbarity of modern warfare. The proclamation of the New World Order has been followed by one war after another, with the US taking the lead in pouring death and destruction on cities halfway around the world. The most modern conventional weapons are used, supplied by companies that boast of their competitive success in selling them. The casualties are overwhelmingly civilians – blown apart by bombs dropped from 30,000 feet, blasted by guns firing thousands of rounds a minute, buried in their homes by rockets and tanks.

When people direct bombs against civilians in the cities of the west, they are denounced as evil terrorists and abhorrent to civilisation. Yet horrors 1,000 times worse are inflicted on civilians elsewhere in the world. Our leaders warn of weapons of mass destruction, while insisting on their right to stockpile nuclear warheads and construct missile systems. People from an Islamic background who turn to religious-based politics in reaction to foreign domination and devastation are denounced, but a US president can launch wars on Afghanistan and Iraq while claiming he obeys the will of God.

Alongside the old horrors of poverty and war, the 21st century brings a new one – climate change. If unchecked, the rise in temperatures caused by greenhouse gases from carbon fuels will melt the polar ice caps, change ocean currents and weather patterns, turn fertile areas to desert, bring crop-destroying storms and flood immense low-lying regions such as Bangladesh, the Nile Delta and Florida. Hurricane Katrina, which came close to destroying New Orleans, gave a foretaste of what to expect. Most of the world's governments admit something must be done, but retreat from measures to curtail emissions lest any group of capitalists lose out.

All these evils have a single cause in the capitalist system. More than two billion people work each day to produce more wealth than there has ever been – more than enough to provide sufficient food for everyone and to overcome poverty. Yet people go hungry in one part of the world while farmers elsewhere are paid to leave fields uncultivated. The organisation of production in a system based on rival companies, each motivated by the drive to compete for profit, is the root cause.

At the top of the biggest companies are a select group of extraordinarily wealthy individuals. There are about 350 billionaires in the world. The top 200 have more than $1 trillion ($1,000 billion) in assets. The three wealthiest are worth as much the 48 poorest countries combined. Such individuals have a controlling stake in the multinational corporations, about 200 of which – run by perhaps 1,500 people – have a combined turnover equal to more than one-quarter of the world output. Of these 200 multinationals, 168 are based in five countries – the US, Japan, Germany, the UK and France. The five biggest, run by perhaps 40 people, have a greater output than the Middle East and Africa combined, and double the output of South Asia.

These few individuals decide what to produce and where, who will have jobs and who will be condemned to poverty. Their economic power gives them enormous political power in countries where they operate, and they pressure states to fulfil their desires – through bodies like the International Monetary Fund, World Bank and World Trade Organisation, and by direct military means. It is capitalism that produces this imperialism, with the ruling classes of a handful of countries – led by the US – prepared to use any barbarity to get their way.

Wherever there is poverty, oppression, war or environmental destruction there are always numbers of people who resist. The 19th and 20th centuries saw successive movements of resistance that gave birth to the ideas of socialism and communism, and the 21st century has already produced fresh movements. There are millions looking for an alternative to the present system and asking questions. What do we do about the power of the billionaires, the corporations and the states that further their interests? Is it possible to overturn that power? Could we rebuild society on a different basis? And how do we avoid the dream of another world turning into a nightmare like Stalin's Russia or simply a repackaged version of market madness?

This book attempts to answer some of those questions by looking at how rulers have been overthrown at various points in the 200 years during which industrial capitalism has come to dominate the world, at the alternatives people have posed to it, and at the possibilities for revolution today.

1:
The actuality
of revolution

R EVOLUTION IS neither possible nor desirable, we are told, except maybe to remove governments which interfere with the running of market capitalism. Yet the 21st century has already seen a succession of near-revolutionary upheavals – the rising that forced the president of Ecuador to flee the country in January 2000, the uprising that drove out the Argentine president in December 2001, the spontaneous insurgency that brought Hugo Chavez of Venezuela back to power after a right-wing coup in April 2002, the uprising that drove out the president of Bolivia in October 2003, the risings that drove out presidents in Ecuador and Bolivia in 2005, and the mass movement that overthrew the government in Nepal in the spring of 2006.

In fact, revolution is so characteristic a feature of the modern capitalist world that the 20th century can be described as a century of revolution. In Europe, alone, there was a revolution in what is now Turkey in 1908; revolutions in Russia in 1905 and 1917; the Irish rebellion of 1916-21; the German and Austrian revolutions that overthrew their respective emperors in 1918-19; and the Spanish revolutions of 1931 and 1936. There were the uprisings that freed Paris, the cities of Northern Italy and

Athens from Nazi occupation in 1944; the East German uprising of 1953; the Hungarian revolution of 1956; the events of May 1968 in France; the Portuguese revolution of 1974-75; the Solidarnosc movement in Poland in 1980-81; and the Eastern European revolutions of 1989-90. Britain is virtually alone among European states in not having fairly recent memories of revolutionary change, and most of the non-western governments represented at the United Nations would not have a seat without the revolutionary movements that ended colonial domination.

The prevalence of revolution should not really surprise anyone. The modern world is shaped by the most rapidly-changing economic system ever known. Its motive force is blind competition to accumulate profit. To this end capitalism continually reshapes agriculture and industry, transforming the conditions under which people make a living, and in doing so continually changes the way in which they live.

At the beginning of the last century 85 per cent of the world's population lived in the countryside, working the land and following patterns of life similar to those of their ancestors. By 2000, half the world's population was concentrated in towns and cities, and it is forecast this will rise to 60 per cent by 2030. This involves a transformation in people's lives greater than any since the development of agriculture during the Stone Age.

REVOLUTION AND THE RISE OF CAPITALISM

Changes in the ways people worked and lived occurred slowly in the societies that existed prior to the rise of industrial capitalism in parts of north-west Europe 250 years ago. Most of the world was dominated by agrarian ruling classes whose wealth came from seizing through rents and taxes one-third to a half of the produce of those who tilled the soil. These ruling classes used various religious ideas to mould the lives of those they ruled into a rigid pattern, encouraging conservative clerics who preached that life would never alter. In the words of a Christian hymn: "The rich man in his castle, the poor man at his gate, He made them high and lowly and ordered their estate."

The rise of capitalism shook these old ways of acting and thinking. A new wealthy class emerged that became rich not through owning land, but through profits from the exploitation of wage labour. This class of manufacturers, bankers and capitalist farmers had different interests and saw the world in different ways to the old landed classes. As the wealth of this class increased, its members tried to impose their vision of how society should be run.

Societies were turned upside down in the centuries that followed. The capitalists challenged the old landowning class economically, ideologically and politically. This process changed the way everyone made a living as well as the institutions that shaped their lives. It was the real reason for the revolutions of the 18th, 19th and early 20th centuries – from the American War of Independence and French Revolution of the 1790s to the Russian Revolutions of 1905 and February 1917.

The new ruling groups consecrated their victories by embracing conservative ideologies of their own, imprisoning people's minds once again with the notion that society is fixed and unchangeable. They encouraged a new array of intellectuals – economists, writers, editors, academics – who declared capitalist values to be part of an unchanging human nature. At the same time, they made peace with the remnants of the classes they had replaced – landowners, lords, royal families, tribal chiefs and religious dignitaries, who were well rewarded for blessing capitalism with the same enthusiasm they had blessed the preceding system of exploitation.

So today we are told from all sides that society cannot be changed. The message comes from popes and pornographers, Christian fundamentalists and sociobiologists, gutter journalists and university vice-chancellors, economists and New Labour politicians. "Compromise, compromise, that is the way for you to rise" is the underlying message to intellectuals – in other words, help put mental shackles on the minds of the majority whose labour keeps society going.

This has its effects. New generations grow up in societies shaped by capitalism. People have never known anything else and take for granted the pattern of life imposed on them, accepting voluntary incarceration at work five or six days a week, 48 weeks a year for 40 years, or languishing on less than $1 a day in a third-world slum. People are rarely very happy under capitalism – you hardly see people laughing with joy on the bus to work or while stuck in a traffic jam. But for periods of time, most people tolerate what the system has to offer. Under such conditions, capitalist notions colonise people's minds – the rat-race mentality, competitiveness, the tendency to blame those of a different ethnic origin, religion, gender or sexual orientation for society's ills. In this way conservative moods can grip not only those at the top of society, but many at the bottom.

THE RESTLESS SYSTEM

Such periods never last indefinitely. The rapidity of economic change produces recurrent social dislocation, to which ideas must adjust. The capitalist system is built on competition between owners of the means of production – small firms in the mid-19th century, giant monopolies and state firms in the mid-20th century, and multinationals today. This competition forces every company to transform production methods continually, closing old workplaces and opening new ones. Towns and cities that grew up around certain industries are decimated. People who live in them find everything they have taken for granted disappears. They have to change the very rhythm of their lives, learning new skills, accepting new conditions, moving to new areas, while never knowing if the changes they make won't also soon be obsolete.

Writing in the *Communist Manifesto*, when industrial capitalism was still in its infancy, Karl Marx and Frederick Engels observed the:

Constant revolutionising of production, uninterrupted disturbance of all social conditions, everlasting uncertainty and agitation distinguish the bourgeois epoch from all earlier ones. All fixed, fast frozen relations, with their train of ancient and venerable prejudices and opinions, are swept away, all new-formed ones become antiquated before they can ossify. All that is solid melts into air.

| 17

This applies more than ever to the present phase of capitalism, usually known as globalisation. Free markets and neoliberalism mean unleashing capitalism from every constraint – including social institutions and attitudes that served it well in the past. Just as people get used to certain ways of working and living, the system throws these into chaos. People naturally expect things to continue in a similar way, but globalised capitalism cannot fulfil such expectations. Every phase of stagnation or contraction throws tens of millions on the scrap heap, and any sober appraisal of the future must see these convulsions only growing as competing units of capital expand to monstrous size.

Half a century ago the defenders of capitalism boasted they had found a way of preventing economic crises and ensuring full employment, rising living standards and expanding welfare services through state intervention. They claimed the economist John Maynard Keynes had shown how to achieve these things in the advanced industrial countries and it was only a matter of time before such developments would spread to the rest of the world. Labour Party politicians in Britain, their social democrat counterparts in mainland Europe and the Democratic Party in the US argued revolution was outmoded because their reforms would create a world of growing prosperity and expanding leisure time.

Today their talk is very different. They declare Keynes out of date and argue problems cannot be cured by state intervention. Now governments react to the ups and downs of the capitalist system by abandoning the methods they once claimed could control the cycle of booms and slumps. Instead of promising a secure future, they say the system depends on the creative destruction of established ways of working. There is no alternative to reforms that expand the scope of the market. Even the most tedious jobs are no longer secure. They tell us jobs for life have no place in the modern world. We must abandon demands for shorter working hours and decent retirement in old age.

CAPITALISM, WAR AND SOCIAL UPHEAVAL

Warfare dominated the first half of the 20th century, with clashes on an immense scale. The period began with Britain at war in South Africa and a struggle between Russia and Japan in the Far East. It concluded with the Korean War involving the US, North Korea and China. The two world wars in between culminated in the Holocaust and nuclear attacks on Hiroshima and Nagasaki.

Through much of the second half of the century it seemed things had changed for the better. The great powers, the US and the Soviet Union, avoided war with one another and their major allies out of fear of mutual annihilation. However, they were no less barbaric than before. The US waged a war in Vietnam that killed millions and backed death squads and torturers across Latin America. Russia crushed an uprising in Hungary and in Afghanistan tried to replicate what the US had done in Vietnam.

The approach of the 21st century brought back old nightmares in a new form. The weapons at the disposal of smaller states were now terrible enough to cause huge death tolls in the wars between Iraq and Iran, Ethiopia and Eritrea, Armenia and Azerbaijan, Serbia and Croatia, and on the eastern borders of the Congo. A single superpower, the US, seized opportunities to show it could out-bomb and out-shoot the rest – against Iraq in 1990-91, Serbia in 1998 and Iraq again in 2003. Other powers, especially Britain, tagged along behind, while France exacerbated the mayhem in parts of its former empire by sending troops to the Ivory Coast in 2006.

This new imperialism is no passing phase. The right to exploit is connected to military might. In the most devastated parts of the world, those seeking increased wealth seize it by force, operating as military entrepreneurs, knowing the accumulation of arms permits the accumulation of capital. At the top of the system, the neo-con group in the US government have set about using the world's most powerful military machine to impose a "new American century". In between, a range of middle-ranking and regional powers see armaments –and above all nuclear weapons – as key to making their voices heard: Britain, France, China, Israel, India and Pakistan. Other states threaten to travel the same path in order to rise in the global pecking order.

Without an alternative to capitalism, wars can only recur and nuclear weapons proliferate. However, war does not only bring suffering. It can shake society to its roots, breaking people from the routine of the past. This can lead to the most reactionary ideas and monstrous behaviour taking hold, but can also result in a questioning of the system that leads to war and to confrontation with the politicians, generals and tycoons who rejoice in it. War cracked seemingly impregnable regimes in the 20th century, bringing the fall of tsars, emperors and presidents. It can do the same in the 21st century.

CONFLICT AND CLIMATE CHANGE

This "best of all possible systems" is destroying the environment we depend on for existence. Capitalism has always functioned by grabbing the cheapest raw materials and pouring out waste products. What this meant in the early days of industrial capitalism in Europe and North America can be seen today in the derelict coal-mining and iron-making areas – the gashes torn in the earth, the stagnant ponds, slag heaps and poisoned soil. Now the system is global, the devastation is global too.

However, the impact is unlikely to be limited to the physical conditions of peoples' lives. There will also be a social impact. People are hardly going to watch their livelihoods disappear without seeking in some way to defend themselves.

Studies of previous societies that appear to have collapsed amid environmental crisis – such as the Mayan civilisations of southern Mexico and Guatemala, and the society on Easter Island in the Pacific – suggest ecological catastrophe was the catalyst for social revolt by the mass of people. Those whose labour had created the wealth to produce palaces and monuments turned on their kings and priests and tore down the symbols of the social system that was destroying them.

Changes in the world's climate in the coming decades

are sure to have an equally profound social impact. Our rulers will attempt to compensate themselves for environmental losses at the expense of rivals in neighbouring states and by increasing the burden on the rest of us. A report for the US Defense Department forecast some possible consequences:

Riots and internal conflict tear apart India, South Africa and Indonesia... Access to water becomes a major battleground. The Nile, Danube and Amazon are all mentioned as high risk... Rich areas like the US and Europe would become 'virtual fortresses' to prevent millions of migrants from entering after being forced from land drowned by sea-level rise or no longer able to grow crops. Waves of boat people pose significant problems. Nuclear arms proliferation is inevitable. Japan, South Korea, and Germany develop nuclear-weapons capabilities, as do Iran, Egypt and North Korea. Israel, China, India and Pakistan are poised to use the bomb [The Observer, 22 February, 2004].

No-one can know precisely the impact of climate change, let alone how this will translate into social and political pressures. What is certain is that there will be pressures. As resources dry up, rival capitalists and states will fight for access to them and ordinary people will try to prevent themselves suffering. All the political and social tensions that characterise the world today will be intensified.

The question is not whether conditions can develop that lead to potential revolutionary upheavals. These are inevitable in a world in turmoil – as economic crises deepen, wars intensify, weapons proliferate and global warming creates havoc. However, there is nothing predetermined about the outcome of such upheavals. The turmoil in the years after the First World War led not to a better society, but to fascism and renewed war.

APATHY AND DISAFFECTION

There is only a minority of people worldwide who accept the need for total social change, despite the growth of anti-capitalist ideas. But the signs of passive disaffection with the present system are visible everywhere.

In virtually every major country, the proportion of people voting in elections has in general fallen over the last two decades. The turn-out in British elections was more than 80 per cent in the early 1950s. In 2001 it was 57.5 per cent, and in 2005 61 per cent – two people out of five could not see a reason to choose between parties offering the same neo-liberal policies. In the US, two-thirds of people did not vote in 2000, and even in the tense election of 2004 more than half stayed at home. In parliamentary elections in France turn-out fell from more than 70 per cent in the 1940s and early 1950s to under 60 per cent in the late 1990s. In Poland, in 2005, the election turn-out was 30 per cent. Only when something appears to be vitally at stake has this downwards trend been bucked – so both the last two French presidential elections have seen high turnouts. In the first the fascist Le Pen had got through to the run-off round for the first time, while in 2007 Sarkozy's hard right-wing platform polarised French politics and voters turned out in large numbers.

Such cynicism about politicians and electoral institutions is not, of course, the same as a desire to overthrow them. But it is an expression of the increasing feeling that the system has little to offer the mass of people. What is characterised as apathy involves a loss of faith in the capacity of existing political structures to do anything for people.

The same passive detachment is demonstrated by the popularity of drugs or the growth of religious cults, particularly in the US. A more dangerous expression of the same thing is the growth in the minority who listen to the rants of neo-Nazis. The 10, 15 or even 20 per cent of people who sometimes vote for such parties are turning away from the monotone message of the mainstream parties and directing their bitterness at people who suffer from the system at least as much as themselves. It is a frightful illustration of how disaffection can turn poisonous if no positive alternative to the rampage of global capitalism emerges.

The key question is whether apathy can give way to consciousness of the need for change among masses of people and the anti-capitalist minority become a majority. Experience suggests such a transformation is possible. Apathy results from a feeling of impotence in the face of overwhelming pressures and a bewildering world. Yet it can switch to its opposite, a commitment to change the world, when individuals become aware that their concerns are shared by many others. It is this which explains the growth of the anti-capitalist and anti-war movements, the wave of uprisings in Latin America and the emergence of new left forces in Europe.

2:
What makes
a revolution?

PEOPLE OFTEN talk as if revolutions are made solely by groups of revolutionaries. Che Guevara famously declared shortly before the CIA murdered him in Bolivia in 1967: "If you are a revolutionary, make a revolution." But revolution never occurs just through the behaviour of a particular group, however big or small. It happens because masses of people, many of whom have never considered the matter before, demand change and put themselves at the centre of political events.

The French Revolution of 1789 began not because of the activity of a handful of republicans, but because thousands of people from the poorest areas of Paris marched on the royal palace at Versailles. The February 1917 revolution in Russia started when women textile workers, sick of working long hours for starvation wages, went on strike and threw snowballs at the windows of factories where their men worked to get them out too. Such events occur spontaneously when vast numbers of working people feel they can only get what they need by taking things into their own hands. Usually, those who have campaigned for revolutionary change are as surprised as anyone by the turn of events.

The Russian revolutionary Lenin, writing in 1915,

pointed to two elements necessary for this transformation in behaviour to occur. First, the lower classes must reach a point where they feel the conditions of life are increasingly intolerable. But in itself this is rarely enough to bring about rebellion. People can react to living standards worsening by becoming demoralised and turning against one another. The amount of grumbling may increase, but not the amount of action.

The second element is that the ruling class gets into such a mess that it cannot easily find a way out. Great economic or political crises do not simply cause increased bitterness at the base of society; they can also provoke the most powerful capitalists to panic – as can a protracted war that cannot easily be settled. Members of the ruling class start blaming each other for what is happening and each capitalist tries to escape the crisis at the expense of rivals.

In extreme circumstances, the propaganda machines and repressive apparatus of rulers can be paralysed. Each section of the ruling class tries to use the media or secret police against its rivals, and each tries to stir sections of the masses to support its plans against its rivals. But even short of such a crisis, fighting within a ruling class can make the mass of people feel they no longer face a wall of resistance to their demands. People who were apathetic suddenly discover they can act.

A revolutionary situation opens up when these splits inside a ruling class combine with rising discontent among the mass of people – when, in Lenin's words, "the lower classes do not want to live in the old way" and "the upper classes cannot carry on in the old way".

REVOLUTIONARY SITUATIONS
Capitalism repeatedly created revolutionary situations in the first half of the 20th century with its wars and economic crises. At the beginning of the 21st century the system is

doing so again. Whole countries, even whole regions of the world, can suddenly be hit by economic crises or military conflicts that make life intolerable for the mass of people and put ruling classes at each other's throats.

Events in Argentina at the end of 2001 offer a prime example of what we can expect in the decades ahead. Through most of the 1990s the country had been a prototype of the globalised national economy. Its president and economics minister were the toast of establishment economists for the speed with which they had deregulated and privatised the economy and welcomed foreign capital. Then Argentina was hit by the backwash from a financial crisis that began on the opposite side of the world. Its foreign debt mushroomed out of control. The domestic market for goods collapsed, unemployment rocketed and the state froze everyone's bank accounts. The ruling class split over what to do. One section wanted to preserve its ability to invest profitably elsewhere in the world by maintaining the exchange rate of the currency against the US dollar. Another section, made up of locally based industrialists and big landowners, wanted the currency devalued so they could sell products more easily on world markets. Their quarrels broke the stranglehold they exercised over the media. An attempt by the dominant section in the government to clamp down by imposing a state of siege, following riots by the unemployed, backfired in the face of general bitterness. People who had never taken to the streets before – government employees, sections of the middle classes – joined manual workers and the unemployed in marching on the presidential palace, fought the police for 24 hours and drove the government from office. The division within the ruling class meant TV channels and newspapers gave expression to some of the bitterness. It also meant the repressive apparatus of the state was virtually paralysed in

the face of recurrent mass demonstrations and as workers took over some of the closed factories.

Argentina has not been an isolated case. We have
seen some of the same elements at work in uprisings in
Albania, Indonesia, Serbia, Ecuador, Bolivia and Nepal.
We can expect many more examples in the years ahead.
A country can appear stable and peaceful for years, only
to discover it has been like a raft on a calm patch of water
between two tidal waves. Under such circumstances, the
mass of people can enter political life in a way no-one
could foresee.

The dynamic of capitalism itself ensures there will be
such uprisings. However, not every uprising results in
revolutionary change. The countries mentioned above
remain largely as they were before the risings. Governments have changed, but the same capitalists run
industry and finance, and dominate agriculture. The
same hierarchies run the armed forces and police, even if
a few individuals have stood down. Obscene levels of
inequality persist and the lives of the mass of people
remain dominated by the insane logic of capitalist markets, even when governments concede small reforms.
Such societies have gone through convulsions – what are
sometimes called pre-revolutionary situations – but these
have not culminated in successful revolution.

UPRISINGS, STATES AND REVOLUTIONS

Revolution involves not just a change of government, but
the turning upside-down of social hierarchies so that a
class previously excluded from power takes over at the
top. In the revolutions during the rise of capitalism this
involved the bourgeoisie – the class with interests tied to
capitalist forms of exploitation – who seized control of the
state from the old landed aristocracy and imposed policies to suit themselves.

The state does not merely comprise parliament and similar institutions. On the contrary, at its core are the armed forces, police, prisons and secret police that constitute the means of repression. These are always organised on a hierarchical basis, so that whatever the social origins of rank and file soldiers, police or jailers, those who give the orders belong to a highly privileged group linked to the dominant economic class.

The end of feudalism culminated in supporters of the bourgeoisie defeating the armies of the old order. The success of the English Revolution of the 1640s depended on Oliver Cromwell creating an army of his own (the New Model Army) and using it to purge Parliament, close down the House of Lords and cut off the head of the king. The French Revolution of 1789-94 involved clashes with troops defending the monarchy (the Swiss Guards), wars against foreign-based armies, the execution of the king, and the use of the guillotine against the aristocracy and its supporters. Industrial capitalism was only established as the dominant force in the US by a bitter war to destroy the armies of the slave-owning plantocracy in the South. In Germany and Italy, wars were required to force disparate local monarchs and princes to accept integration into modern capitalist states.

However, these revolutions involved more than just the conquest of the state. Society could only be overturned in its entirety if there was also a transformation of economic relations and of the values which shaped people's lives. There had to be economic and ideological revolution as well as political revolution. These changes took place over a much longer time than the political revolutions. But the new class could not consolidate its rule without seizing state power.

The origins of capitalism go back to the 13th and 14th centuries, with groups in parts of Europe slowly increasing their economic power through capitalist forms of exploitation. As their economic power grew, so did their capacity to influence ideas – through the development of printing and bookselling, the sponsorship of churches, the endowment of universities. However, this did not rule out the need for a culminating moment of conquest by armed force.

Where such a conquest did not occur, there was the likelihood of the old ruling class using its armed might to destroy the economic power of the emerging capitalists and to terrorise people into accepting the old ideology. This happened at the end of religious wars in the 16th and 17th centuries in Germany, France, Austria and the Czech lands, during which the bourgeoisie fought under the banner of various versions of Protestantism and the old ruling classes under that of Catholic counter-reformation. The bourgeoisie lost the military battles to change the state and was forced to submit to the old order for a century or more. This happened again after France's defeat by the other European powers in 1814-15, although the setback was more short-lived. It would have happened in England in the 1640s, France in the 1790s and the US in the 1860s if Cromwell, Robespierre or Lincoln had held back from a full-blooded assault on the forces of the old order. In each case, revolution was a drawn out process, but one which reached a point when sudden and decisive action was necessary.

There is a difference between the situation of workers under capitalism and that which faced the bourgeoisie under feudalism. Those exploited under the present system cannot gradually accumulate economic control. There are those who dream of establishing workers' or peasants' cooperatives to challenge capitalism, but these have no chance of long-term success. The capitalists control all the accumulated fruits of the exploitation of previous generations. While workers' cooperatives may, on occasion, demonstrate that production can take place without capitalists, they do not provide a means of countering the enormous resources in the hands of billionaires and multinational corporations.

This means the question of who controls the state is even more important today than during the bourgeoisie's ascent to power. If the bourgeoisie were defeated by the armies of the old order, they could still exercise influence through their continuing ownership of property. But when the capitalists succeed in smashing the struggles of the classes they exploit – by breaking strikes, imprisoning trade unionists, driving peasants from the land – these classes are left with nothing to resist further attacks. They face economic subjugation as well as political subjugation, and inevitable demoralisation. People lose faith in the possibility of replacing capitalism and succumb to the idea that there is no alternative. Worse, the defeated can turn on one another and scapegoat members of ethnic and religious minorities.

3:
Parliamentarianism and revolution

THE PLAYWRIGHT George Bernard Shaw, in his play *Man and Superman*, wrote: "Every general election is a revolution." He was expressing the widespread assumption that, under capitalism, power lies in the hands of elected parliaments or presidents. We commonly hear that a politician has "taken power" following an election. Yet this is mistaken.

The origins of the British state go back to the Middle Ages, with its modern form shaped to suit the needs of capitalism in the 17th, 18th and 19th centuries. There was no democracy in Britain in the early 19th century. Parliament was chosen by a tiny minority – 95 per cent of the male population was excluded from voting until 1832, 80 per cent remained excluded after the reform of that date, and women did not get the vote until the following century. Democracy was anathema to those who ran the British state at the time. They denounced it as "mob rule" and the masses as "the swinish multitude". The British historian Macaulay wrote in the early 19th century, "Universal suffrage would be fatal for all purposes for which government exists" and "utterly incompatible with the existence of civilisation".

Mass pressure forced extensions of the franchise, but it was not until after the First World War that something approaching universal suffrage was conceded in Britain – and even then some women had no vote and some upper class men more than one. However, the extension of the vote did not change the fundamental character of the state. In his book *Capitalist Democracy in Britain* (Oxford, 1982), Ralph Miliband wrote:

The politicians' appropriation of 'democracy' did not signify their conversion to it: it was rather an attempt to exorcise its effects... A carefully limited and suitably controlled measure of democracy was acceptable, and even from some aspect desirable. But anything that went beyond that was not. The whole political system was geared to such sentiments.

WHERE POWER REMAINS

The army, courts, security agencies and civil service were run very much as before, with the same hierarchies in control. At the top were the relatives and friends of those with great economic wealth – and the situation has not changed. Studies of the officer class in the armed forces, the judiciary and the top ranks in the civil service show 80 per cent of their members attended the top fee-paying schools. The occasional police chief from a lower middle class or working class background can expect to be honoured with a lucrative position upon retirement.

The rank and file of the state machine must obey these people unquestioningly. A Whitehall civil servant or prison officer who refuses to toe the line will lose their job. A soldier who disobeys an order faces military prison. They are trained to obey orders and face punishment if they forget that training - and it is those above them in the hierarchy they are trained to obey, not MPs voting in parliament.

What is true of Britain is true of every other country in the world. If most of the officers of the armed forces come from the middle rather than the ruling class, as sometimes happens they are still organised as a caste apart from rank and file soldiers. They live in special accommodation, eat special food, have rank and file soldiers as servants, and enjoy a career that promises most to those who stick closest to the rules. Such people might sometimes fall out with sections of the ruling class, but they rarely forget what divides them from the mass of people.

At elections, voters do not get to choose who will hold economic power. That does not change. So there is no democracy when it comes to economic decisions – about what to produce, how high to fix wages and who has a job. Elections do not alter the character of the state. Even if a left-wing president or a majority of left MPs are elected, the generals, police chiefs and judges remain in place, along with the industrialists and bankers, and society continues running along capitalist lines. Those at the top may go through the formality of implementing decisions by elected bodies, but they do their best to sabotage such measures they dislike, using every excuse not to damage the interests of the capitalist class while that class uses its economic power to force the government to cave in to its demands.

IT HAS HAPPENED HERE

In 1974 a Labour government was elected in Britain that promised to reduce inequality by "squeezing the rich until the pips squeak". The phrase was that of a leading Labour right-winger, Denis Healy. The capitalist class reacted with fury. A top industrialist, Sir Frederick Catherwood, announced an "investment strike". Lord Watkinson boasted of the "industrial muscle" of big business and its ability to confront the government. Major firms and banks began to move money abroad. *The Sunday Times* described the resulting sterling crisis as the "logical climax of the mood of hysteria necessary to produce an agreed incomes policy" that would cut wages. A follower of the markets told the newspaper: "It looks as if they [industrialists] are putting the frighteners on."

Those in the hierarchies of state did their best to aid big business in its battle. Joe Haines, press secretary to the prime minister of the day – Harold Wilson – later described the behaviour of the heads of the civil service:

From 1974, Defence fought to spend more against Labour's commitment to spend less; Environment waged war against the railway system when Labour was pro-railway; and the Treasury persuaded the government to retreat from its commitment to a wealth tax. The determination of the Treasury to tell the government to accept policies is ruthless, even to the point where it seeks to create conditions which make it impossible for the Cabinet to spurn its advice.

Journalist Peter Jenkins described in the *Guardian* how he had been told by "an authoritative foreign source" that the Treasury was using the sterling crisis to pressurise the government. "They are constantly in touch with our people saying, 'Don't bail these bastards out'."

There was no way the Labour government could address the crisis through the exercise of its parliamentary majority alone. It did not control the state machine, and the state machine did not control big business. Harold Wilson was like a weakling in the ring with a champion heavyweight boxer. The only way to stop being pummelled was to surrender. A Labour government that had come to power promising reforms to improve the lives of working class people ended up pushing through the biggest cuts in real wages for half a century.

This has not just happened once. It was the experience of Labour in Britain in 1929-31 and 1964-70 as well as

1974-79, the Socialist-led Popular Front government in France in 1936, the coalition governments of France and Italy at the end of the Second World War, and of the Mitterrand and Jospin governments in France in the 1980s and late-1990s. On each occasion, high hopes of reform gave way to bitter disillusion and discredited right-wing parties seized the opportunity to make a comeback.

The only exceptions to this pattern of blackmail and betrayal came in the 25 years after World War Two. The 1945-51 Labour government in Britain and similar governments in Scandinavia were responsible for some reforms of considerable benefit. However, this was an extraordinary period for capitalism – what some refer to as its golden age. Massive spending on arms, especially by the US, fuelled a world economic boom and governments were able to work with big business to ensure more-or-less continual growth. Profits rose to such an extent under these conditions that employers could afford to give way to pressure for improved wages and welfare services. This was not just true of countries with Labour-type governments – it happened in conservative-run countries like France, Italy and West Germany, and in the Tory Britain of the 1950s and early 1960s.

That era is long past. Capitalism today is dominated more than ever before by giant multinationals that reach out from their national bases to manufacture and trade around the world. Governments cannot control the tempo of individual economies under such conditions, however much they collaborate with big business. All they do is dance to the rhythm of the wider system as it gyrates wildly from booms to sudden slumps. But keeping up with the dance involves telling workers to accept reforms of a very different kind – signifying longer working hours, less secure jobs, lower unemployment benefit and reduced pensions.

The word neo-liberalism signifies the rebirth of what used to be called 'liberal capitalism' in continental Europe and 'free market' or 'laissez faire' capitalism in Britain and the US. It culminated in the great economic crisis of the inter-war years.

Governments run by those who claimed to be able to reform capitalism proved helpless in the face of that crisis. In Britain, Labour prime minister Ramsay MacDonald told his party's conference in 1930 there was little his government could do. "So my friends, we are not on trial. The system under which we live has broken down, not only in this little island; it has broken down in Europe, in Asia, in America; it has broken down everywhere as it was bound to break down." In Germany, the former social democratic finance minister Rudolf Hilferding admitted, "We are unable to tell the people in a concrete manner how we will eliminate the crisis." Too much was "out of the hands of German social democracy, out of the hands of anybody", he said.

Instead of running capitalism, they found capitalism was running them and leading to disaster. A year later MacDonald abandoned the party to run a Tory government. Ten years later Hilferding committed suicide to avoid torture and murder at the hands of the Nazis. There is no reason to believe governments operating today under the re-born, free market capitalism can be any more successful.

BITTER LESSONS

There are those who argue popular pressure can stop left governments caving in so easily – and mass pressure can certainly have an impact. It can be so great that not only governments, but the state and big business give ground before it. Members of the ruling class can feel similar to the Tory Quentin Hogg (later Lord Hailsham), who told his party conference in the middle of World War Two: "If we do not give reform, we will get revolution."

Faced with mass strikes in 1936, the French ruling class allowed the Popular Front government to push through reforms. So did the Chilean ruling class when faced with the huge upsurge of agitation that followed the election of Salvador Allende as president in 1970. A US-backed attempt at a coup failed miserably late in that year. But on both these occasions, the ruling classes and their state gave ground only temporarily, to play for time. By 1937-38 the French ruling class was compelling the Popular Front's parliamentary majority to undo the reforms passed in 1936 – and in 1940, parliament voted for collaboration with the Nazi occupation under Marshall Petain. In Chile, the ruling class went further and took armed action to impose its will. After a year or more of economic sabotage designed to turn a section of the population against the government, there was a military coup. In September 1973 General Pinochet moved tanks into the major cities, bombarded the presidential palace – killing Allende – and arrested and murdered thousands of government supporters. Allende had appointed Pinochet head of the army only two months earlier.

In the aftermath of that coup, many of those who supported changing society by working through the existing state – including the leaders of the Italian Communist Party and the British historian Eric Hobsbawm – drew a strange conclusion. They argued the mistake in Chile had been to go too far, too fast, and concluded the only way a reformist government could stay in office was by abstaining from implementing the reforms people wanted. It was an admission that you cannot bring the kind of changes we need to society through the existing state. If another world is possible, we will not reach it through such methods.

This does not mean we should simply ignore parliaments. They are the focus for what most people see as politics and provide the terrain on which arguments about the direction of society take place. When people want to tackle a social ill, they usually look to parliament to do it. So although election results cannot, in themselves, produce serious social change, they can be a measure of people's desire for change – and make individuals aware of the degree to which others share their desire.

An election campaign can help pull together those who want to change society and offer a chance for them to present their ideas. Success in electing even a single MP or deputy can give a platform for a radical position that can influence the opinions of millions. This was the case in Germany at the beginning of World War One when the revolutionary socialist Karl Liebknecht used the parliamentary chamber to make a stand against the war, breaking the wall of silence imposed by state censorship. It was also what happened in Britain in the late 1960s and early 1970s when a young socialist from Northern Ireland, Bernadette Devlin, used her election to parliament to denounce repression by the British state. Most recently, in 2005, the election of George Galloway as Respect MP for Bethnal Green and Bow provided an opportunity to take the argument against imperialist war to the heart of the US government – the Senate.

Parliament is a debating chamber in which, at its best, representatives of different classes, with different notions of what society should be like, can air their views in public. A debating chamber cannot overturn the hierarchies of power embodied in the state, but it can provide a means for mobilising people against those hierarchies.

However, even when there is a left-wing majority in parliament or a left-wing president, such a mobilisation depends on what happens in the streets and workplaces.

This was shown in a negative sense in Chile in the early 1970s. It was shown in a much more positive sense in Venezuela in April 2002 after a group of generals staged a coup, kidnapped the twice-elected president, Hugo Chavez, and installed the head of the employers' federation in his place. Millions of the poor of Caracas surrounded the presidential palace two days later, leading a section of the armed forces to turn against the generals and restore Chavez. Six months later, mass action by the country's workers stopped a second attempt to overthrow the president during a management shutdown of industry.

Had it been left simply to those in parliament, Chavez would not have survived and Venezuela would have gone the way of Chile. The country's poor would not have gained the subsequent reforms paid for from booming oil revenues, and there would be no talk in Venezuela of "socialism in the 21st century". As it is, the country's rich are forced to tolerate reforms out of fear of a renewed mass movement, while biding their time in the hope that the workers and the poor forget how the coup was thwarted.

4:
Revolutionary democracy

EVERY GREAT revolution has depended upon people exercising power through institutions much more genuinely democratic than elected parliaments and presidents. People have tried to create forms of organisation subject to their continual control, knowing that they could not simply rely on voting once for a representative to act on their behalf in face of the powerful forces trying to preserve the old order.

This was true even in the bourgeois revolutions. At the height of the English Revolution of the 1640s, the soldiers of the revolutionary New Model Army, drawn from the lower classes, elected delegates known as "agitators". They were briefly able to force the wealthy grandees who commanded the army to listen to some of the demands from below and to push through the revolution. In the French Revolution of the early 1790s, the lower classes of Paris – the *sans culottes* – met in each district to enforce their demands on the city council and on the revolutionary convention that ran the government.

However, these experiences proved transitory. Once the rising middle class had sufficient power to subordinate the old feudal interests to their control, they crushed the revolutionary democracy, preferring to revert to monarchical government rather than see their economic power threatened by a democratic mass movement.

The first great attempt by workers to take power, the Paris Commune of 1871, produced a much greater extension of revolutionary democracy. Following a war with Germany that saw the French army crushed and Paris besieged, the workers of the city took control and established a commune. They elected delegates from each district to represent them, making them subject to recall at any time and paid no more than the wage of a skilled worker. They implemented decisions themselves rather than turn to an unelected hierarchy of bureaucrats, and relied not upon a professional or conscript army, but on the armed workers, organised as a national guard.

New forms of revolutionary democracy began to emerge in the working class revolutionary upsurges of the 20th century – the workers' councils. The first was born in October 1905, during strikes that came close to destroying the 400-year-old Tsarist Empire. Striking print workers in the capital St Petersburg elected delegates to form a council, or soviet in Russian, and delegates from other striking factories joined them. The council became the organising centre of a movement that held the city in its grip, a focus for the economic and political demands of the oppressed classes and, in effect, an alternative government to that of the Tsar.

DUAL POWER

This set the pattern for what was to happen in every Russian city in 1917, when mass strikes and demonstrations led the army to mutiny. The Tsar abdicated and was replaced by a government committed to capitalism and to keeping Russia in the First World War. However, workers' and soldiers' councils emerged overnight from the mass movement and gave organised expression to the growing anti-war and anti-capitalist feelings of the mass of people. For eight months there was a state of "dual power", with the councils acting virtually as a workers' government challenging the prerogatives of the official government. In October 1917, the majority in the workers' and soldiers' council in the capital took power into its own hands – a decision immediately ratified by a congress of the workers' and soldiers' councils across the country.

A similar situation developed in Germany a little over a year later when strikes and mutinies overthrew the empire of the Kaiser. Again there was dual power, with an official government seeking to maintain capitalist rule, and workers' and soldiers' councils taking many day-to-day decisions. But this time the official government won out, using sections of the old officer corps to smash the revolutionary movement in a succession of localised civil wars.

Delegate bodies of armed workers played a similar role in the Spanish revolution of the summer of 1936 after mass uprisings had defeated General Franco's military coup in more than half the country's cities. These committees organised the militias which fought a civil war against Franco and at the same time began to take over sections of the economy – a story told in George Orwell's book *Homage to Catalonia* and Ken Loach's film *Land and Freedom*.

When Hungarian workers rose against Russian occupation in 1956, workers' councils again became their organising tool. In the first place, delegates were elected from factories in different localities to organise the struggle against the occupation and ensure food and basic services were provided. But the councils soon began to coordinate their efforts to provide the beginnings of a government from below.

Peter Fryer went to Hungary to report for the *Daily Worker*, the paper of Britain's Communist Party, and was subsequently expelled from the party for the honesty of his reporting. In his book *Hungarian Tragedy* (London, 1997) he wrote:

In their spontaneous origin, in their composition, in their sense of responsibility, in their efficient organisation of food supplies and civil order... and not least in their resemblance to the workers, peasants and soldiers councils which sprang up in Russia in the 1905 revolution and in February 1917, these committees, a network of which now extended over the whole of Hungary, were... at once organs of insurrection – the coming together of delegates elected by factories and universities, mines and army units – and organs of popular self government in which the armed people trusted.

Even after Russian troops crushed the armed uprising, the Central Budapest Workers' Council operated as an alternative government in the city for several weeks, until its members were arrested.

In Chile, in the last months of 1972 and early 1973, delegates from factories in the industrial belt of the capital Santiago began to play a somewhat similar role in committees known as *cordones*. The left-wing government was under increasing attack from capitalist interests, with the barely concealed support of sections of the state machine. When the employers attempted to close down industry, in a kind of bosses' strike, workers set up factory committees to keep industry running and supply their communities with food. In drawing the different committees together through the *cordones*, they created the beginnings of a popular government network.

The experience was repeated in the Polish city of Gdansk in 1980. Workers occupied a shipyard to resist the sacking of a female activist and to demand improved wages and conditions. Workers in 250 other workplaces joined in and together they created a delegate body, the "Inter-enterprise strike committee" (MKS). In his history of the struggle, Colin Barker wrote:

The whole movement was based on a huge wave of workplace occupations. Each striking enterprise sent a delegate to its local MKS. The delegates elected an inner executive committee under this immediate control. The major negotiations with the state were conducted in front of microphones, which were linked to the shipyard tannoy system so that thousands of workers could follow the proceedings... Delegates returned to their workplaces with tape recordings of the proceedings, to report and renew their mandates... Within days of its establishment the Gdansk MKS had begun taking control of essential services in the area [Colin Barker, "Poland, 1980-81: The Self-Limited Revolution" in Colin Barker (ed), *Revolutionary Rehearsals*, London, 1987].

For 16 months there were two powers in Poland. There was the official government, which controlled the army and police but had little support among the population, and there was the network of workers' organisations, now calling themselves a trade union, Solidarnosc, but in practice more like workers' councils than any union (by contrast, when Solidarnosc reformed in 1989 it was as an old-style trade union, lacking any mass-based workers' democracy).

Workers played the key role in each of these movements. But the momentum drew in much wider layers of society. In Russia in 1917, Germany in 1918-19, Spain in 1936, Hungary in 1956 and Poland in 1980 similar democratic forms of organisation spread to encompass all sorts of groups – soldiers, peasants, teachers, intellectuals, sections of the lower middle class and oppressed minorities. Once one section of the exploited and oppressed showed it had the power to fight back and reshape its existence, it drew all sorts of other sections behind it and began to unite the whole of society. In doing so, these movements began to show in practice how society could be rebuilt on a new basis. In each case, people of all sorts began to consider how to make a different world.

WHICH CLASS DICTATES?

As Karl Marx saw it, every class society involves a dictatorship of the ruling class over the rest of society. Sometimes this dictatorship is exercised by a despot. Sometimes it is exercised through a form of democracy restricted to the ruling class. So in the Roman Republic the slave-owning upper classes exercised their dictatorship "democratically" through a senate to which they alone had access. In the southern states of the US before the Civil War, slave owners decided among themselves how to exercise control over their slaves.

In modern capitalist societies, control of the economy and the state by a small ruling class amounts to a dictatorship over the rest of society, even when it is tempered by the granting of political rights to the masses. In each case, one class rules over another.

Revolution involves turning the situation upside down, so the exploited and oppressed rule. It means the working class becoming the ruling class. This is the sense of a phrase Marx used – "the dictatorship of the proletariat". He meant that the working class would organise democratically to impose its will on those who previously held power. This would be something more democratic than parliamentary democracy, not less so. It would involve replacing the existing authoritarian state with institutions directly accountable to the mass of society, and these would take over economic as well as political decision-making. Marx argued such institutions would arise as the mass of the population organised themselves to counter the violence of the existing state, and would reorganise society as a whole in the interests of the majority. Frederick Engels pointed to the Paris Commune of 1871, with its elected delegates subject to recall, to illustrate in practice what working class rule – the dictatorship of the proletariat – would look like. Where the Commune led, the workers' councils of the 20th century would follow, providing a taste of the kind of revolutionary organisations we can expect in the upheavals ahead.

5:
Class and revolution

REVOLUTIONARY SOCIALISTS believe the working class is the key to transforming society. This follows from the character of capitalist society. Capitalists cannot survive without making profits, but they cannot do that without bringing workers together to exploit and thus creating discontent. This is what Marx meant when he wrote that capitalism creates its own "gravedigger".

Ruling classes before capitalism also exploited the mass of the population. But they did so mainly by exploiting peasants dispersed across the countryside, each family tending its own land, living in villages or hamlets with little connection between them, speaking localised dialects, unable to read and write, and possessing little understanding of the wider world.

Capitalism, by contrast, concentrates those it exploits in giant cities, in workplaces where improved conditions can only be obtained through collective struggle. In order to exploit workers to the maximum, capitalists demand a level of literacy and numeracy higher than that among most of the exploiting classes of the past. In doing so, the system creates a class with the capacity to organise against it and the potential to turn society on its head.

THE REALITY OF CLASS TODAY
The revolutionary movements of the 20th century were

centred on the industrial working class. Innumerable academics and media pundits argue this makes workers irrelevant to the question of revolution today because the working class has declined as a force. If there is talk of demands for change it is couched in terms of "multitudes" and "social movements".

There is no doubt the proportion of people employed in manufacturing and mining has declined in Britain and certain other advanced industrial countries. The number in manufacturing in Britain today is about half that of 1973. But this does not mean the industrial working class has disappeared – its numbers were still growing in the US until only six years ago and even in Britain there are still millions of such workers. More importantly, the notion of the working class cannot be restricted to those in particular industries.

The media, politicians and academics treat class as a question of lifestyles or, following the German sociologist Max Weber, "life chances". Their starting point is the way people dress and speak, the character of the jobs they do, the degree to which they are held in esteem or extent to which they live in poverty. This leads to the assertion that we live in an increasingly middle-class society, since the proportion doing heavy manual work has declined while increasing numbers work in white-collar, service sector jobs. We live in a "two-thirds, one-third" society, it is claimed, in which most people prosper and a minority make up an "underclass".

Many on the left see class in similar ways – identifying a "labour aristocracy" of skilled, male manual workers and an impoverished underclass, or portraying industrial manual workers as "proletarian" and white-collar and service-sector workers as middle class.

These theories obscure the fact that the fundamental divide in society is between those who control the means of production and those who work for them. Lifestyle, dress, income and consumption are products of this division, not its cause. It is irrelevant if occasional members of the possessing class choose to slum it, or if some of the toilers gain marginal advantages and imitate aspects of the lifestyle of their exploiters. The fact that the head of Barclays and a counter clerk in a branch of the bank both wear suits does not bridge the gap between them. The bank clerk, computer operator and call centre employee are compelled to accept voluntary wage-slavery, five days a week, 48 weeks a year, just as much as a car worker or docker.

RESTRUCTURING AND THE CONTINUITY OF CLASS

The competition at the core of capitalism means firms repeatedly restructure production to try to get ahead of rivals and to survive recurrent crises. This leads to the repeated restructuring of the labour force. Some groups of workers diminish in size and others expand. So in Britain in the 1830s and 1840s the biggest concentrations of workers were in textiles. When people thought of the typical worker, they thought of someone in a cotton mill. Forty years later, whole new branches of industry were expanding and people increasingly identified the working class with those in heavy industry – the shipyards and mines. By the Second World War things had changed again, with a great expansion of jobs in the car industry, electrical goods and light manufacturing.

At each stage people looked at the changing lifestyles of those around them and concluded the militant working class of the past was gone. Around 1870 Thomas Cooper, a former activist in the Chartist movement 30 years earlier, surveyed the workers of the north of England and:

noticed with pain that their moral and intellectual conditions had deteriorated...In our old Chartist times, it is true, Lancashire working men were in rags by the thousands; and many of them lacked food. But their intelligence was demonstrated wherever you went. You would see them in groups discussing the great doctrines of social justice... they were in earnest dispute respecting the teachings of socialism. Now you will see no such groups in Lancashire. But you will hear well dressed working men talking of cooperative stores and their shares in them, or in building societies. And you will see others, like idiots, leading small greyhound dogs, covered with cloth, on a string...Working men had ceased to think... [Quoted in Max Beer, *A History of British Socialism*, 1940].

Some 70 years later the idea that the old working class had disappeared became fashionable again. A broadsheet of the government's Central Office of Information declared in 1962 that British society was characterised by a "swelling middle class". There could be no return to the working class conditions of the 1930s because: "The average man...has made too great an investment in his own future as a middle class citizen and householder" (quoted in John Goldthorpe, David Lockwood and others, *The Affluent Worker in the Class Structure*, Cambridge, 1969).

There was a serious academic discussion as to whether "affluent" car workers were "embourgeoisified". Labour Party theorist Anthony Crosland wrote:

One cannot imagine today a deliberate offensive alliance between government and the employers on the 1921 or 1925-6 model, with all the paraphernalia of wage cuts, national lockouts and anti-union legislation; or a serious attempt to enforce a coal policy; to which the miners bitterly objected [CAR Crosland, *The Future of Socialism*, London, 1956].

Yet a wave of workers' struggles began in the late 1960s, culminating in confrontations that shook society as much as those of the 1920s, forcing a Tory government out of office in 1974. At the heart of the militancy were supposedly affluent workers in the car, mining and printing industries. And the militancy was not finally destroyed until the defeat of the miners in a year-long strike in 1984-85 that involved the police occupation of the mining areas.

The restructuring of industry changes the working class and confuses observers, but it cannot do away with the central features of capitalism that lead to recurrent waves of class struggle.

THE WORKING CLASS IN THE 21st CENTURY

The restructuring of capitalism in the advanced countries is characterised by two trends: a growing proportion of the workforce is made up of white-collar workers, and service employment is growing more quickly than industrial employment. The trends should not be confused. Many service jobs are manual (bus drivers, dockers, refuse collectors) while a considerable proportion of manufacturing employees are white collar (progress chasers, design office staff). But the trends can give a misleading impression of what is happening to the class structure if you identify the working class solely with manual industrial workers.

What has not changed, despite all the transformations in work brought about by restructuring, is the fact that the system is based on competition between rival firms. This leads companies to do their utmost to pump the maximum profit out of their workforce. As a section of workers grows in size, then the pressure on them to produce profits increases.

When white-collar work was the prerogative of a

relatively small number of male clerks in the 19th century, capitalism could afford to provide them with better salaries and conditions than the mass of manual workers. But 21st century capitalism depends on vast numbers of white-collar workers doing routine jobs. Many work for private firms in banks, insurance companies and advertising agencies. Others are employed by the state to carry out functions important to the system as a whole – training the next generation of workers, collecting taxes, protecting property, keeping people fit for work. These workers are exploited through the same methods as manual workers. Job evaluation methods pioneered in the textile mills, steel plants and on car assembly lines are applied to civil servants, teachers and even university lecturers.

One consequence of this change is that such groups now engage in characteristically working-class forms of struggle. In Britain, strikes by teachers, civil servants, lecturers, journalists, nurses and white-collar workers in local government were virtually unknown until the late 1960s. They have become as normal as strikes by old-style manual workers in the last 30 years.

Modern capitalist society is divided into two main groups as clearly as the 19th society analysed by Marx or described in the novels of Charles Dickens. There is a small minority who have enough wealth to live a life of leisure if they wish, and there is a great mass of people who can only make a livelihood if they work for this minority.

This division is more important than any other in society. It determines how much control you have over your life – whether you enjoy real choices or whether everything you do is subordinated to the need to work for others. It even determines how long you are likely to live, with the employing class in Britain today expecting to live, on average, more than 10 years longer than the rest of us. It determines the quality of the clothes you wear, the car you drive, the food you eat and the goods you own. All the factors usually taken to indicate class are effects of this division. Analyse Britain according to this basic division and you find well over 75 per cent of people are working class, in the sense of depending for their livelihood on selling their labour to the minority.

Not all service employees or salaried staff are workers. In any society there are gradations between the small minority at the top and the mass of people at the bottom. In a slave society there are not just slave owners and slaves, but also a layer of slave drivers, who receive a small share of the wealth that comes from exploiting the slaves. In a capitalist society, there are a mass of small capitalists and self-employed business people as well as the major capitalists. There is also a layer of managers, top civil servants, police chiefs and so on who are paid much more than the value of any labour they perform in return for helping big capital exploit the mass of people.

This layer is organised through bureaucratic hierarchies. Those at the top partake fully in the fruits of exploitation and have common interests with big capital. Those at the bottom get very little from exploitation and share many interests with the white-collar and manual workers below them. Low-grade supervisors and line managers are paid a little more those they order around, but rely on the same public services and can be hit just as hard by workplace closures and redundancies.

The presence of this middle layer obscures the basic divide between the exploiting and exploited classes. But it does not do away with it any more than the slope between a hill and a valley does away with the contrast between the two. Far from making up the majority of society, this middle class proper amounts at most to 15-20 per cent of the population.

Another argument you hear about workers today is that globalisation has created such massive insecurity in employment that it is all but impossible to develop the strong workers' organisations that existed in the past. Far from workers being able to challenge the state, they find themselves barely able to fight an individual employer.

This argument suffers from two inter-related faults. First, workers have often succeeded in organising and fighting back against employers despite massive levels of job insecurity. Take the case of London's dockers in 1889. This was a group with no security of employment. Gareth Stedman Jones' book *Outcast London* quotes the findings of a parliamentary select committee on conditions in the docks in 1888:

Bribery and favouritism were the normal means of gaining employment in the docks. Treating the foreman to beer on the evening before was a frequent means of gaining employment in the docks the next day. Casuals in the docks applied daily for dock work at gates where they were known by the foreman. This could not assure them a day's work, since the foreman always employed a proportion of outsiders in order to increase the size of the casual pool. On the other hand, the foreman could punish long term absence on the part of the casual workers by withdrawing his patronage. It was this precarious dependence of the casual upon the foreman that maintained the casual fringe intact.

Beatrice Webb, one of the founders of the reformist Fabian Society described the position of dock labour in 1887 as "very hopeless". "The employers were content and the men, although far from content, were entirely disorganised," she wrote.

Conditions were not much more secure for metal and

textile workers in the Russian capital St Petersburg at the end of 1904. According to historian Gerald Surh:

The turnover within the factory workforce in Petersburg seems to have been quite high... Unskilled and semiskilled workers were normally more volatile because they were more easily replaced...The lack of organisation and therefore protection at the workplace meant that the inevitable dispute between workers and foremen and managers were... frequently resolved... by resignation or dismissal [Gerald Surh, *1905 in St Petersburg*, Stanford, 1989].

In both cases, mass strikes transformed the situation and encouraged hundreds of thousands of other workers to throw up new organisations of their own. When the London dockers struck in 1889, they shut down the city's international trade for five weeks, won their economic demands and built a union of 25,000 members. Beatrice Webb highlighted the change:

What the men had achieved through organisation was not to be measured solely by advantage achieved in pay or the conditions of employment... We see the effect in the changed attitude of the employers as to casual employment.

In Petersburg, the transformation was even more dramatic. The unorganised workers of 1904 exploded into action after management victimised a woodworker in the Putilov plant. As Surh writes: "A mass meeting of 2 January, attended by about 6000 workers... enthusiastically voted for a strike at the Putilov plant... By Friday 7 January, 382 enterprises were on strike." When the Tsar's troops fired on a peaceful demonstration, the strike spread across the city and began a year of revolutionary upheaval that came close to overthrowing the regime.

Such a sudden discovery of the power to fight back collectively can occur among the restructured working class of the 21st century. We have already had glimpses of it. In the forefront of the uprisings in Bolivia in 2003 and 2005 were workers from the mass of small workshops in the city of El Alto. The spring of 2006 brought sudden, unexpected strikes and riots in the giant textile factories of Bangladesh, and January 2007 saw strikes and factory occupations by workers in Egypt.

Capitalist restructuring can certainly decimate old-established sectors of industry and weaken the power of groups of workers that used to be among the best organised, as happened with the defeats of the miners and newspaper printers in Britain in the mid-1980s. But the same restructuring leads to a growth in the importance of new groups. Neither the postal workers nor London tube workers were regarded as militant or powerful in Britain in the 1970s, but they have become so in recent years. We can expect other groups, at present largely unorganised — like those working in finance, call centres and supermarkets – to follow at some point. The very logic of capitalism creates discontent among those it exploits and oppresses, and at some point this bitterness will explode. The key question is not whether it will happen, but whether it will prove successful.

The second major fault with the argument that precarious employment prevents workers from struggling is that, in most countries, it is a minority of workers who are in casual jobs. A study by the International Labour Organisation concludes:

While this type of employment increased substantially during the first half of the 1990s, the relative proportions of permanent and non-permanent jobs remained almost unchanged between 1995 and the year 2000: permanent (82 per cent), non-permanent (18 per cent).

The average conceals large divergences between countries, with a high point of 35 per cent of workers in insecure employment in Spain. In Britain, according to the government statistical publication *Social Trends*: "As many as 92 per cent of workers held permanent employment contracts in 2000 as compared with 88 per cent who did eight years earlier."

Even in third world countries such as India and Pakistan, where millions of workers move each year from the countryside to cities seeking work, there is relative security of employment for some sections. Employers like to have a stable element in their labour force, to stop other employers poaching experienced workers when trade is booming and to encourage workers to identify with their particular firm in a way that discourages militancy. After all, it is a positive benefit to an employer if workers say, as a shop steward in a Leeds factory once told me: "This is the best firm in the country." There has been an increase in casual employment in some countries in recent periods of economic crisis. But it is not an unstoppable trend in capitalism as a whole, and it certainly will not stop workers organising and rocking the system.

GLOBALISATION AND WORKERS

It is often argued workers cannot fight back as they once did because the globalisation of the world economy allows firms to shut down operations and re-open somewhere else. Globalisation certainly means finance houses and speculators can move massive amounts of money from one country to another at the click of a computer.

There is also a trend for firms in one country to buy into those in other countries. But it is harder to move production from country to country than it is to move money. Productive capital is made up of factories and machinery, mines, docks and offices. These take years to build and cannot simply be carted away. Sometimes a firm can move machinery and equipment. But this is usually an arduous process and, before equipment can be operated elsewhere, the firm has to recruit and possibly train a sufficiently skilled workforce. In the interim, not only does investment in the old buildings have to be written off, there is no return on investment in the machinery.

What is more, few productive processes are ever completely self-contained. They depend on inputs from outside and links to distribution networks. So before a firm sets up a car plant it has to ensure there are supplies of quality steel available, secure sources of nuts and bolts, a labour force with the right level of training, reliable power and water supplies, a trustworthy financial system and a road and rail network capable of shifting finished products. It has to persuade other firms or governments to provide these things, and the process of assembling them can take months or years of bargaining. Multinational companies do not simply throw these assets away and hope to find them thousands of miles away because labour is slightly cheaper or governments slightly more co-operative. Such moves take time and effort and involve writing off costs. Productive capital simply cannot be as footloose as people often suggest.

The claim that firms find it easy to move production overseas is widespread in the US. But economist Tim Koechlin reports that less than 8 per cent of US productive investment goes abroad. Job losses are mainly the result of firms cutting the number of workers they employ in existing plants, or closing some plants so as to concentrate production in those that remain.

In Britain, the pattern is much the same. The manufacturing workforce has been cut in half over the last 30 years, but total output has not fallen and each worker is producing twice as much as 30 years ago. In other words, each worker is more important to the system now than in the past. There are many important jobs that cannot be moved abroad – for example, in construction, newspaper printing, the docks, the civil service, post and telecommunications, local government, education, refuse disposal, food distribution and supermarkets. Even in the case of call centres, where some work has moved to India, employment in the sector in Britain continues to expand.

Of course, firms do shift location and investments do not always occur in the same places. Restructuring often does involve moving production to a new area, and sometimes to another country, and this is likely to increase in the decades ahead. But such decisions incur costs and are never taken lightly. Firms that are restructuring usually prefer to act gradually, moving piecemeal from old plant to new, keeping supply and distribution networks intact and minimising dislocation. In the process, workers retain the power to stop production and to fight attempts to make them pay for restructuring.

The most important effects of the movement of money from country to country are that it increases economic instability and makes people feel more insecure. Firms often play on this, threatening to move production abroad when they have little intention to do so, in the expectation that this will demoralise workers and persuade them to accept deteriorating conditions. In calling the bosses' bluff, workers can begin to discover their capacity to fight for a world without insecurity.

6:
Class and
consciousness

THE WORKING class comprises the majority in society, it has the power to shake the system, and it will recover eventually from the combination of defeat and restructuring, however much its composition may have changed.

Unfortunately, this does not mean most of its members have a clear idea of their ability to replace the existing system with a better one. On the contrary, being brought up in capitalist society leads most people to accept the ideas of the system to a greater or lesser degree – its racism, sexism, competition and greed, and the belief that there is no other way of living. This is what Karl Marx meant when he wrote that "the ruling ideas are the ideas of the ruling class."

Working class organisations such as the trade unions simply do not control the resources necessary to compete during normal times with the capitalist media. In such periods only a minority of people accept ideas that challenge the system as a whole. The majority take most things for granted and accept much of what the capitalist media say.

It is only when those whose labour keeps capitalism going are engaged in fighting aspects of the system that they discover they have the power to paralyse it. Only then do large numbers begin to see clearly that their interests run in opposite directions to those of the capitalists. They discover through struggle that they can challenge the system, and that as a class they have an interest in uniting to replace profit making and competition with a society of democratic self organisation. It is through struggle that people discover they have the collective capacity to change society.

CONTRADICTORY CONSCIOUSNESS

Antonio Gramsci, a key figure in the history of revolutionary socialism in Italy,* explained that most workers have a "contradictory consciousness". On the one hand, they are brought up in capitalist society and take many of its notions for granted. On the other hand, they have experiences of collective struggles in which they stand together and change the world a little to their own advantage. Some of these experiences are direct ones they have had personally. Others are conveyed from one generation to the next within workplaces, communities and organisations such as trade unions. Workers who have never been on strike before take up the language of solidarity, of unity and respect for picket lines, and the use of terms like "scab" for those who break a strike. So the mind of the average worker contains elements that look to the future and the values of collective struggle and organisation, as well as elements that pull back to the past, towards class society and its prejudices.

The number of people open to the idea of changing society grows massively during great struggles. Mass

---

*   His ideas have been distorted by reformist politicians and academics
     since his death in 1937 for purposes he was adamantly opposed to.
     See my pamphlet, *Gramsci versus Reformism* available at www.isj.org.uk

strikes and spontaneous uprisings lead to an unprecedented level of discussion about what to do next. For the first time people feel their capacity to change things. Politics is talked about everywhere – in every bus queue, shop, factory and office, in every school and at every social gathering – in a manner inconceivable during non-revolutionary times. I have vivid memories of France in May 1968 and Portugal in 1975 when people devoured socialist newspapers the moment sellers appeared, and how in Argentina in 2001-2 people gathered at scores of local popular assemblies to discuss what to do next.

Disgust at the present system allied to experience of striking and demonstrating together makes workers particularly receptive to the notion that collectively and democratically, they can take charge of society themselves. Socialist ideas fit with working class experience whenever people get involved in struggles.

However, revolutionary socialist ideas are not the only ones on offer. The newspapers of the ruling class use the old methods of divide and rule – scapegoating members of ethnic or religious minorities, spreading lies about socialists, trying to turn those not involved in struggle against the groups that move first. For example, in Russia in 1905 after the strikes and formation of the first soviet the Tsarist government worked with the far right in an attempt to deflect the movement by encouraging a series of pogroms against Jews. Today we not only see a revival of struggles against the system, we also see an onslaught against religious and ethnic minorities – Islamophobia in Europe and the US, attacks against Shia Muslims and Christians in Pakistan, agitation against immigrants from Bolivia and Paraguay in Argentina, a witch-hunt against asylum seekers in Britain. People can react to these horrors by turning to notions that make it seem that religion, not capitalist exploitation, is the central fact of the world we live in. So while revolutionary socialist ideas can grow in the ferment against the system, they have to be fought for. There is always a battle of ideas.

REFORMISM

There have always been those who balance between support for capitalism and opposition to it. They say society should be changed in a non-capitalist direction, but slowly – through negotiations and legal processes, not direct confrontation. This was the approach of "Old Labour" in Britain and the Social Democratic parties in mainland Europe.

Such reformist ideas are encouraged by politicians who make their careers by presenting themselves as champions of the workers within the existing order. They have adjusted their lives to arguing for progressive reforms within the existing state and inevitably try to channel any upsurge against the system in this direction. Sometimes this is because they have come to accept many of the values of the ruling class. Sometimes it is that they have so adjusted to fighting for reform that they cannot imagine any alternative. In either case, they try to tame the movement so as to stop it challenging the state. Their efforts are reinforced by sections of the media who implore all classes to work together.

However, this reformism should not be seen merely as something imposed on the mass of people, who would otherwise be revolutionary. It flows from the position of any subordinate social group in a class society as its members try to bridge the contradictions in their consciousness between the ideas they have absorbed from that society and those which come from their acts of rebellion. Reformism is the organised political expression of contradictory consciousness, which is used by politicians for their own purposes.

THE TRADE UNION BUREAUCRACY

Reformism is not just embodied in political parties. Trade unions are also pulled in a reformist direction. The whole structure of capitalist society springs from people's labour. To challenge the way this is provided – at work – means, implicitly, to challenge that structure. By organising people at work, trade unions begin to raise questions about the very foundations of society. This is what Lenin meant when he said any strike raises the "hydra head of revolution".

But people's capacity to work (what Marx called their labour power) is also a commodity within capitalism. It is bought and sold by the hour just as apples or tomatoes are bought by the kilo. Haggling over the price of labour power can seem no different to bargaining over the price of any other transaction in the market, encouraging the notion that what matters are presentation skills and administrative structures – the professional negotiator rather than the revolutionary agitator. So the union apparatus becomes an institutional structure within existing society, run by its own specialist functionaries. It has the double role of organising workers and bargaining with capitalists over the terms of employment. It mediates with employers on behalf of workers.

This kind of trade unionism appeals to workers insofar as they have not broken from the ideas of capitalist society. It seems to offer the reformist hope of improving conditions without the requirement for revolutionary action. However, the appeal is not only to workers – it is also to groups of capitalists. Any ruling class faces contradictory pressures of its own. It wants unlimited power to exploit and dominate the rest of society, but crude force alone is not sufficient to stabilise that exploitation and domination. The need arises for mediating structures that draw in elements from among the mass of people.

As both Lenin and Gramsci put it, a ruling class needs institutions that give it hegemony as well as domination.

For example, the feudal ruling classes of medieval Europe usually ended up allowing a section of the merchant and artisan classes to establish limited forms of organisation – in guilds and town corporations. They granted those who ran these a subordinate, but honoured, position in the social hierarchy, understanding this would lead to acceptance of the hierarchy as a whole. This worked for decades, even centuries, at a time. The most successful merchants sought to buy their way into feudal society, not overthrow it.

Capitalists usually start off opposing all attempts by workers to organise, and some groups of capitalists never abandon this outlook. But others learn that a resentful workforce can be volatile and prone to sudden, disruptive action. They see the need for mediating structures to bind workers' organisations to the system – hence, the wooing of trade union officials with various honours. The former leader of the print workers' union, Brenda Dean, now sits in the House of Lords, and the former leader of the transport workers' union, Bill Morris, is on the board of the Bank of England. This need also explains the attacks by the media and the courts on trade union leaders who challenge this cosy relationship – as miners' leader Arthur Scargill did during the great strike of the 1980s. This carrot-and-stick approach shapes the trade union bureaucracy to accept the system – whether individual trade union leaders do so reluctantly or enthusiastically.

The trade union bureaucracy comes to take this mediating role for granted. It evolves a career and salary structure that mirrors the managerial hierarchies of business and develops a reluctance to engage in any confrontation that might threaten the union apparatus, property and salaries. In a classic history of trade unionism

Sidney and Beatrice Webb described the change among workers in Britain who became union officials:

Whilst the points at issue no longer affect his own earnings or conditions of employment, any disputes between his members and their employers increase his work and add to his worry. The former vivid sense of the privations and subjection of the artisan's life gradually fades from his mind and he begins more and more to regard all complaints as perverse and unreasonable. With this intellectual change may come a more invidious transformation. Nowadays the salaried officer of a great union is courted and flattered by the middle class. He is asked to dine with them, and will admire their well-appointed houses, their fine carpets, the ease and luxury of their lives... He goes to live in a little villa in a lower middle-class suburb. With the habits of his new neighbours he insensibly adopts more and more of their ideas. Gradually he finds himself at issue with his members... He attributes the breach to the influences of a clique of malcontents, or perhaps to the wild views held by the younger generation [Sidney and Beatrice Webb, *A History of Trade Unionism*, 1894].*

The Webb's account has been vindicated many times. In 1926 one of the most important episodes in the history of class struggle in Britain took place – the General Strike. At that time one in ten industrial workers in Britain was in the coalmines, whose owners announced they would lock out and refuse work to any miner who would not accept a cut in wages and longer hours. The Conservative government backed the mine owners, declaring all workers had to accept wage cuts.

The country's union leaders, gathered in a special meeting organised by the Trades Union Congress, made ringing declarations in support of the miners and called for all trade unionists to strike – first transport workers and then other sections. Millions of workers did so and Britain was paralysed. But the union leaders were far from overjoyed. Some, like rail union leader Jimmy Thomas, were as frightened by the strike as the government and big business. Thomas told TUC leader Walter Citrine: "The strike is against the state and the state must be supreme." He later wrote: "what I dreaded most was this: if by any chance it should have got out of the hands of those who knew how to exercise some control." The leader of the general workers' GMWU expressed a similar attitude:

Every day the strike proceeded, control was passing out of the hands of responsible executives and into the hands of men who had no authority, no control, and was wrecking the movement from one end to the other.

These leaders manoeuvred alongside the government to deny victory to the class from which they came. They brought the general strike to an end after nine days, despite there being no loss of momentum; in fact numbers on strike grew by 100,000 24 hours after the TUC called it off. The TUC left the miners to fight alone for nine months before surrendering to face longer hours on poverty pay or unemployment. Other employers were left with a free hand to sack workers who had organised the strike at a local level.

Almost 60 years later, the miners' strike of 1984-85 unfolded in a shockingly similar way. The miners fought desperately for 12 months against a programme of pit closures that was to devastate the industry and their communities. There were glowing declarations of support from trade union leaders at the 1984 TUC Conference, while behind the scenes leaders of some unions outside the mines sabotaged solidarity with the miners and undermined the strike. The head of the Coal Board, Ian MacGregor, who led the onslaught against the miners, wrote later: "There were a number of union leaders with whom I could communicate and talk frankly". The result was the second great defeat of the century for Britain's trade union movement – a defeat to be followed by two decades of demoralisation and union weakness.

However, responsibility for these defeats did not just lie with the leaders who allowed themselves to be bought by the capitalist class. It also lay with union leaders of a more honest disposition who were unwilling to break with the rest of the union leadership and encourage the rank-and-file to carry the struggle forward. When it came to the crunch, they were as little inclined to see the struggle through to the end as their pro-capitalist colleagues. After the 1926 General Strike, Jimmy Thomas – the rail union leader who did so much to sabotage it – reported that a left wing leader of a second rail union had been just as keen to end the strike.

What was true of these decisive battles is also true of many lesser struggles over pay or redundancies. Full-time trade union officials are part of an apparatus committed to negotiating on behalf of ordinary workers – pressing claims on management, but also persuading workers to accept whatever concessions management might make. It results in an emphasis on the negotiating skills of union officials rather than the fighting spirit of the union members and seeks escape routes from confrontations with employers. Again and again, it has meant sacrificing the union members in an effort to preserve the union apparatus – although a union that cannot defend its members is inevitably damaged as the workers will see no reason to belong to it.

This is not the end of the matter because a structure that seeks to mediate between classes is subject inevitably to tensions, which pull first one way and then another. Discontent among workers repeatedly throws up new activists who challenge the conservatism of the bureaucracy. Even right-wing bureaucrats can see that they mean nothing to the employers unless they can channel and express some of the discontent below them. So they switch between opposing any form of industrial action to calling strikes in an effort to maintain their influence, and from witch-hunting militant activists to trying to incorporate these into the union hierarchy. At the same time, union elections ensure that there are always some individual officials who want to fight for the interests of ordinary members.

Yet the conservative tendencies remain. The bureaucracy that calls a strike to show its influence will call off the action at the first opportunity if its position is threatened either by rank-and-file initiative from within or by repressive threats from without. Left-wingers within the bureaucracy then suddenly find themselves isolated, unable to use the levers of the union to keep the struggle going. It is this that explains the tendency for the right wing to run from the battlefield in any great confrontation, pulling the centre behind them and leaving the left feeling helpless to operate on its own.

THE CONTRADICTORY ROLE OF REFORMISM

The growth of reformist parties and trade unions constituted a gain for workers as they came to understand their position as a class within capitalist society, with interests opposed to other classes. The building of the social democratic parties in continental Europe in the 1880s and 1890s, the Labour Party in Britain in the first quarter of the 20th century, or the more recent growth of organisations such as the Workers Party in Brazil, all represented a step forward compared to the previous situation, when workers backed openly capitalist parties. But the advance is only a partial one. Such parties try to restrain workers from confronting the real sources of capitalist power and the state even whilst organising them as a class. They both hold the class together and hold it back at the same time.

Reformism could gain deep roots in the working class during periods of economic prosperity, when it seemed capitalists could increase their profits while conceding improved living standards. The reformist parties and moderate wings of the trade unions could recruit hundreds of thousands of activists to build working class organisation – but who did not see any logic in fighting to overthrow the system. So in the decades immediately after the Second World War in Western Europe most socialists and many who called themselves Communists accepted the idea that there was a parliamentary road to socialism. Allegiance to the reformist parties remained strong even when capitalism began to demand counter-reforms from conservative governments that took away the improved living conditions that had been previously granted. However little the reformist parties promised, they seemed a "lesser evil".

Yet frequently, it has been Labour and social democratic governments that have pushed through the counter-reforms in the past decade, doing enormous damage to workers' allegiance to them. Millions of voters have turned away from the Labour Party in Britain and the Social Democratic Party in Germany, and hundreds of thousands of members have dropped out of these parties. Many now abstain from politics, but a substantial minority have begun to look for a new, left-wing form of politics represented by the Left Party in Germany, Respect in Britain, the Left Bloc in Portugal, the vote for the various far left parties in France, and the new PSOL party in Brazil.

People who break with the old reformist parties do not necessarily make a clean break with reformist ideas. Bitterness against the current leaders of such parties does not in itself lead people away from reformist to revolutionary notions; they can still believe reformist methods would work with better leaders. But the bitterness is leading them to organise and mount political resistance alongside those people who do embrace a revolutionary perspective. The new left politics provides a focus for resistance and a political space in which people who share a common opposition to the system can seek to resolve the debate about reform and revolution.

7:
The role of
revolutionaries

REVOLUTIONS NEVER break out just because of the efforts of groups of socialists, however dedicated. They occur, as we saw, when great social crises create a situation in which "the lower classes do not want to live in the old way" and "the upper classes" are "cannot carry on in the old way". The current stage of capitalism, globalisation, has led to greater unpredictability and uncertainty for the ruling classes, and greater suffering for the oppressed in whole regions of the world – making it inevitable there will be great social crises in the century ahead of us. The dynamic of capitalism ensures that upheavals will take place.

But not every situation of this kind ends in a socialist revolution, far from it. Most of those we have referred to in the last century did not. More recently, the uprisings in Ecuador, Argentina and Bolivia have so far replaced openly neo-liberal governments with those promising progressive reforms. This is because the contradictions in people's consciousness do not simply disappear even during periods of upheaval. People have it hammered into their heads that they can't run things. So, even after overthrowing a government, most people are likely at first to place their hopes in a new government, apparently less hostile to their demands.

Even as millions of people discuss how to change society, the influence of ideas and institutions that argue for only limited reforms persist. While whole groups of workers with past experience of struggle move beyond notions of reform to see the need to confront the system, other groups making their first moves towards class consciousness tend to follow the trade unions and reformist parties which tell their supporters to hold back from a revolutionary confrontation. This reformist approach – sometimes coated in radical, even revolutionary language – always finds a mass audience in the period after a first popular upsurge.

In fact, solutions that avoid confrontation are not possible during social crises on this scale. But that does not prevent many people seeing the reformists at first as more practical and less violent than those pushing for revolution. After the uprising that overthrew the Tsar in Russia in February 1917, people put their faith in governments headed first by a war profiteer, Prince Lvov, and then by a lawyer, Kerensky, committed to maintaining capitalism intact. In Argentina in 2001-2 people who threw out four presidents from the old political establishment, one after the other in less than a month, eventually came to tolerate two others from a similar background – Duhalde and Kirchner.

What seems like a single, spontaneous movement on the day of the first upsurge, always develops into different currents – in effect, three parties, whether they use this name or not; a revolutionary party, a reactionary party and, attempting to bridge the gap between them, a reformist party.

There are sincere revolutionaries who oppose the existence of parties at all arguing that they undermine the spontaneous self-activity of workers. But any genuine mass movement involves a wide array of people with differing views on what needs to be done. Many argue for the line of action they think correct. Someone suggests a demonstration or strike. Someone else thinks such action is premature and there should be further negotiations. A third person wants no action at all. A movement may appear spontaneous to an outside observer but viewed from the inside it invariably involves attempts by myriad individuals to lead in different directions.

Parties would come to exist even if the divergences between people were simply random, but they never are. The divergences are structured by the pressure of existing society on the protests that arise – above all by the assumptions engrained in the people's consciousness that things cannot be fundamentally different to the past. Conservative currents argue society cannot be changed at all and reformist currents that it can only be changed in part. These currents form spontaneously through the impact of existing society, and are encouraged by the media and by those with careers tied to the existing political institutions. So when people say there is no need for parties, they are saying that there is no need for revolutionaries to get together to oppose these currents.

However, the outcome of a revolutionary situation depends on the outcome of the battle by these different currents to give direction to peoples' bitterness. In conditions of great crisis, where the reformist option can provide no solutions, the battle increasingly becomes a straight fight for influence between revolutionaries and reactionaries. The future comes to depend on whether those who have abandoned hopes for reform turn to revolution or reaction.

The battle is both one of ideas and a practical struggle. The ruling class relies for its supremacy on the working class being fragmented and lacking in confidence. Workers can only overcome such impediments through the experience of struggling for control in the workplace and on the streets. The momentum of struggle at such times can give even the most unpolitical workers a sense that they are part of a movement that can create a new society. Reformist attempts to slow the movement then can prove disastrous, breaking the feeling of strength and allowing fragmentation to return along with the reactionary ideas of the ruling class.

This was shown tragically in the case of Chile. The attempt of the ruling class to smash the reforms of the Allende government in 1972-73 provoked a counter-offensive by workers. But there was a powerful reformist current in the workers' movement, centred on the Socialist and Communist parties and in control of the national union federation. Its leaders argued the army generals would respect the constitutional powers of the president and that the most important thing was not the struggle in the factories but winning elections and the support of the supposedly more moderate of two pro-capitalist parities, the Christian Democrats. When workers took to the streets against an attempted coup in June 1973, fraternising with soldiers, a minister in the Allende government told them to go home and rely on the loyalty of the generals to the constitution. This gave the generals time to re-establish their hold over the rank and file of the armed forces and to prepare the barbarously successful coup of September 1973. The generals then murdered the minister.

Revolutions invariably reach a point at which they must either move forward, or begin to slip back. Going back can mean a return of the old order in a worse form even than before. The only way to prevent this is for revolutionaries to be organised to present their ideas and suggest a different way forward. A revolutionary party is not necessary to start a revolution, but it is essential to ensure its victory when the choice is between socialism and barbarism.

8:
Building the party

WHAT SORT of organisation constitutes a revolutionary socialist party? There are two widespread conceptions, both of which are mistaken. One is that the party should be based on electioneering, like the Labour Party but more left wing. It builds its strength through propaganda until it has enough parliamentary seats to form a government, or at least a coalition with other left-wing parties. This was the approach of the first Marxist party in Britain, the Social Democratic Federation, more than a century ago, and it is an approach that persists today in organisations such as the Communist Parties of France and India, the Socialist Party in the Netherlands and the United Left in Spain. The problem is that great social crises involving masses of people are not fought out in parliament or according to parliamentary timetables. Electoral activity can provide socialists with an important way of putting across their ideas but it cannot substitute for waging a struggle in workplaces and on the streets.

The second conception is of a tightly organised group that tells workers they need a revolution and that it will make one on their behalf, believing workers will turn to it when the situation becomes desperate. But it keeps clear of daily struggles in case this creates illusions in the possibility of reform. This was the view of the 19th century French revolutionary Blanqui and of one of the most prominent Italian Communists of the early 1920s, Bordiga. It was also the approach of some of the left-wing guerrilla groups that flourished in Latin America in the 1960s and 1970s. In many ways it is a mirror image of the electoral approach, sharing the notion that revolutionaries must change society on behalf of the mass of people – the masses have only to provide passive support, whether for a left MP or a revolutionary fighter.

The genuinely revolutionary approach is different. It starts from the recognition that a break with the horrors of class society can only occur if the mass of workers take power in their own hands, and that the only way they can gain the strength and understanding to do so is through their own struggles.

Only at times of social crisis and revolutionary upheaval can the majority of workers be won to the arguments of revolutionaries. Yet there is always a minority who can be won to revolutionary socialist ideas outside of periods of upheaval because capitalism continually pushes people to rebel. They may join a strike over wages, a campaign against housing privatisation, a protest against racism, or a movement against war. At any point there will be scores of struggles and in each of these some people will begin to challenge the priorities of the system. A genuine revolutionary organisation attempts to draw these people together to help clarify their ideas through discussion, learning from the experiences of past struggles, analysing the system and the struggles of today, and feeding the conclusions back into the day-to-day struggle.

The aim is to create a network of the most militant people to reinforce each other's strengths, compensate for each other's weaknesses and learn from each other's experiences. Members of the network can act together in the different struggles, drawing these together and countering any attempts to turn one group of workers against another.

This is important even when the level of struggle is low. Each defeat weakens workers, making it easier for reactionary ideas that scapegoat minorities to take hold. Each victory makes it more difficult for the ruling class to subdue workers and the poor completely. But when struggle reaches a high pitch, the existence of a revolutionary organisation with a network of activists in every workplace and locality can be vital. The outcome of major battles can determine the character of the class struggle and the ideological atmosphere for years. So the memory of May 1968 in France still gives right-wing politicians nightmares today, while the memory of the defeat of the miners in 1984-85 still dampens the class struggle in Britain. The building of networks of socialists is a necessity if future struggles are going to win.

Many people are suspicious of self-proclaimed vanguard organisations. But the reality is some workers have a clearer idea of what capitalism is and the need to fight it than others. They are the people who stand up against racism or sexism, see the need for solidarity with any group fighting back, and want to fight to win. In these ways they are ahead of other workers in political consciousness and need to organise together to win others to fight against the system effectively.

PARTIES AND WORKERS' COUNCILS

There is no contradiction in saying we want to see society run by workers' councils and stressing the need for a revolutionary party. The central point about workers' councils is that they represent all workers, not just those who have been revolutionaries or trade union militants in the past. In Russia in 1905 and 1917 the workers' councils were the means by which workers from very different political backgrounds could decide together what they needed to do and set about doing it. Someone who had accepted Tsarist propaganda until the February Revolution could feel just as involved in framing the demands of their class through the workers' councils as someone who had been a revolutionary opponent of the Tsar for a quarter of a century. The workers' councils enabled all sorts of workers to begin to feel they had the power to determine how to run society.

However, these changes did not take place at the same speed among all workers. Many continued to be influenced by the ideas inculcated in them by the old system. In every workplace there remained workers influenced by Russian nationalism, by anti-semitism and by traditional attitudes towards women. Above all, even workers who felt they should be able to influence the direction of society often accepted that they were not capable of running things themselves. So, at first, the middle class and moderate socialist politicians who wanted to maintain Russia capitalism got a big following among workers and won the majority in the workers' councils.

The experience of the months of upheaval led many workers to change their minds – but only when that experience was distilled through daily arguments with those who saw the need for a further revolution. This is where the Bolshevik Party came in. Lenin and the people around him were known as the hard faction among socialists in Russia in the years before 1917. They were disdainful of amateurism and vague thinking. They insisted two things were essential to make the Russian Revolution a success – the development of clear ideas, and a relentless struggle to connect with every workplace and locality through a network of party members. The Bolsheviks were not afraid to be unpopular when occasion demanded – as when they stood out firmly against the war in 1914. But they were certainly not a small, conspiratorial group run like a religious cult by Lenin. They attempted to build as widely among workers as the situation permitted. So in the years 1912-14 they took advantage of a brief relaxation of censorship laws to establish a best-selling workers' newspaper.

The Bolsheviks formed a small minority in the early spring of 1917, but they grew out of the struggles which pitted workers against the new government until they had more members among workers in the main cities than all other parties combined. Bolshevik members were not robots who simply followed Lenin's commands. Lenin often found himself in a minority and had to win people to his views through vigorous debate. For example, Lenin was isolated to begin with when he returned to Russia from exile in 1917 and argued the Bolsehviks should oppose the new government. He was only able to win the rest of the party to this view because workers in the key Vyborg industrial district agreed that what he said made sense.

In autumn 1917 one of Lenin's oldest collaborators, Zinoviev, spoke out publicly against the overthrow of the government sparking a huge debate within the party. Three months after the October revolution Lenin and Trotsky argued with packed meetings that the revolutionary government should accept savage terms from Germany for ending the war.

The party was not something outside the workers' movement and workers' councils. It was the means by which the most militant section of workers argued about polices and sought to win the others to their implementation. If the Bolshevik party had not existed, the parties that sought to tie workers to capitalism would have succeeded and the workers' councils would have been drowned in blood – as they were in Germany barely 18 months later.

STRATEGY, TACTICS AND
THE PARTY OF A NEW SORT

The struggle takes many forms. For long periods it involves what Antonio Gramsci called a war of position – a long, drawn out fight to make a slow advance. During this period, revolutionaries engage in hundreds of little battles – in trade union struggles, fighting against welfare cuts, anti-racist campaigns, building solidarity with strikes and campaigning at elections – to try to improve the condition of the working class a little and to win a few more people to revolutionary ideas.

Such actions in themselves leave capitalism intact while building the network of people who want to overthrow it. These networks only come into their own when the war of position gives way to what Gramsci called a war of manoeuvre – sudden, rapid confrontations in which the mood of millions of people can change overnight. If a revolutionary organisation is strong, its members can point vast numbers of people in the direction necessary for society as a whole to move forward. If it is weak or non-existent, people's hope can turn to despair and everything goes backwards.

The class struggle is a form of warfare, even if for long periods it is a low intensity war. Both sides use strategy and tactics to try and gain a winning position. This is certainly true of the ruling class. At business association meetings, in exclusive clubs, at meetings of the G8 or European summits, in the columns of newspapers and magazines, such as the *Financial Times* and the *Economist*, members of the ruling class discuss how to create the conditions for profitability to rise, and how to beat back the inevitable resistance. Groupings of ruling class interests emerge that win the backing of the rest of their class for various measures designed to lull the resistance into passivity or to isolate one section from the rest, or split it down the middle. Through secret meetings and memos these groups pressure governments, top civil servants and police chiefs to act accordingly.

A revolutionary organisation rooted in the class struggle has to develop strategies and tactics to counter such manoeuvres. It has to identify the weak points in the resistance and do its best to overcome these, and must try to locate the weak points on the ruling class side. Sometimes it is simply a question of trying to hold people together in the face of a defeated strike or a demonstration smashed up by the police. Sometimes it is a question of seizing an opportunity to go on the offensive presented by a new confidence among workers and divisions within the ruling class. Often it is a question of winning a handful of people to the possibility of revolution, occasionally it is a question of leading millions of people in a direct assault on the power of the ruling class. There is no single set of tactics or slogans appropriate to every situation. These have to be worked out at every point in the struggle, and the revolutionary organisation has to operate in such a way as to put them to the test, to see which ideas work in practice.

This has important consequences. The organisation cannot be a loose federation of activists, each doing what they want without reference to one another. Their actions have to be coordinated, to provide a coherent response to the ruling class in an ever-changing struggle. This requires a degree of centralisation in the organisation, a willingness to come to decisions and to implement them collectively. It also necessitates democracy, as the only way to ensure decisions really fit the experience of members involved in different struggles.

In mainstream political parties there is always a separation between a leadership that works out policies and a membership that implements them. In the Labour Party tradition there is a further separation between those who engage in politics through the party's electoral activity and those who engage in economic struggles through the unions. The revolutionary organisation aims to overcome both sorts of division. In the words of those who took part in the great revolutionary wave at the end of the First World War, it is a "party of a new sort". It seeks to fight on every front – the economic, the political and the ideological – just as the ruling class does. It tries to mobilise at work and in the unions over political issues – against war or to oppose fascism – and sees ideological and theoretical debate not as something for academics, but as part of the process of clarifying issues for everyone involved in struggle. At the same time, the organisation does not neglect even the most elementary issue concerning wages and conditions in work, refusing to leave such issues to the reformism of the trade union leaders.

THE UNITED FRONT

The most important tactical question for revolutionaries concerns working with those workers who are influenced by reformist ideas. It is easy when someone first becomes a revolutionary to be dismissive of people who continue to have faith in reformist politicians or trade union leaders. After all, this means accepting parliamentarianism and the existing state and the idea of partnership with employers. But to refuse to work with such people is to turn your back on them and to abandon the class struggle.

This became a central issue for revolutionaries in the years immediately after 1917, when revolution had been victorious in Russia but failed in Germany and Italy because the majority of workers still looked to reformist leaders. It was a central issue again in the 1930s, when the spread of fascism threatened the existence of all working class organisations. It is central today when there is a growth of resistance to the system, but most of the world's workers, peasants and poor people are far from accepting revolutionary socialist ideas.

The essential method for dealing with this, developed in 1917 and the years following it, was the "united front". It rests upon the recognition that people who look to reformism want things that capitalism will not give without a struggle, and that reformist leaders will usually hesitate about leading such struggles. What people want can vary hugely from wage increases to the withdrawal of wage cuts, from protection of public services to political rights or an end to an imperialist war. In every case these are things that revolutionaries as well as reformists favour, and they cannot be won by revolutionaries alone.

In the 1930s, for example, fascism was a threat to every form of working class organisation as well as to Jews and other minorities. Hitler banned the Social Democratic Party as well as the Communist Party and dissolved the trade unions. The only way to defeat the Nazis and forestall the Holocaust and world war would have been to mobilise the strength of the entire working class. Tragically, it did not happen.

Similar considerations have applied since 2001 in the struggle against the wars waged by the US with British support. Revolutionaries oppose such wars out of principle, but our numbers alone would have no impact on the governments waging them. It is only by campaigning alongside vast numbers of people who do not share revolutionary views that ending the wars in Iraq and Afghanistan becomes a possibility.

Such unity cannot be built on ultimatums and preconditions. You cannot build unity against fascism if you work only with those who agree to oppose all capitalist governments. The demands around which a united front is established should be acceptable to people with reformist ideas, even when these are the minimum desired by revolutionaries.

Something else is important. To win large numbers of people to engage in joint struggle, when they still have faith in reformist politicians or trade union leaders, requires a call for united action to be addressed to those leaders, even though they cannot be trusted. The call has to be along these lines: "You say you stand for opposition to war. So do we. Let us fight together." If the leaders agree, we have a better chance to achieve the goal of the campaign and an opportunity, working alongside those who look to these leaders, to demonstrate the superiority of a revolutionary approach. If the leaders reject the call, it should be easier to win their followers away from such influence than if the call were never made.

Pursuing a united front does not mean revolutionaries dropping their disagreements with reformist leaders, who invariably attempt to backtrack on the struggle necessary to win. Revolutionaries must aim to persuade large numbers of people to carry the struggle forward if the reformist leaders refuse to do so. That means continuing to put revolutionary arguments in newspapers, leaflets, public meetings and individual discussions while engaged in united action.

How the united front is formed depends on concrete circumstances. Obviously, it does not make sense for revolutionaries to seek a united front with New Labour against a war waged by Tony Blair, or one against cuts in public services made by New Labour in government. But there should be attempts to involve Labour and trade union figures in united action on such issues, even though they disagree with revolutionaries on much else. This is how the Anti Nazi League was built in the late 1970s and a similar approach has been essential to the success of the Stop the War Coalition since 2001.

One final point: reformism does not always take a form associated with the Labour Party or trade unions. Movements can arise over single issues and not see a connection between that issue and capitalism as a whole. Building a united front may involve an approach to such movements or to well-known individuals identified with them. This is especially important in the struggle against racism. The issue is always how to draw people who do not accept revolutionary ideas into united struggle.

9:
Capitalism
and violence

THE ANTI-CAPITALIST columnist George Monbiot has articulated an argument you often hear. Writing in the *Guardian* in May 2000, he wrote "If advanced capitalism is the most violent of all political systems then violent conflict with that system is bound to fail." Such arguments are usually combined with claims about the success of non-violent direct action movements in the past, like those of Martin Luther King and Mahatma Gandhi. However, neither example lives up to the claims made for it.

Martin Luther King's movement did use non-violent tactics. But the aim was not to convert the segregationists of the US South and the Ku Klux Klan. Rather, it was to persuade the US government to intervene against the segregationists, using an embodiment of organised violence, the US federal forces. When this tactic ceased to work the Student Non-Violent Co-ordinating Committee broke with King and adopted the slogan of armed self defence.

Gandhi represented one element in a broad liberation movement, most of which was prepared to use violence if it seemed necessary. The highest point of struggle, the Quit India Movement of 1942, included strikes, armed attacks on police stations, the derailing of trains, bombings and riots. One of the Indian leaders, Bose, established an army to fight on the Japanese side against the British. The final action that persuaded the British to abandon the country was an Indian naval mutiny in Bombay in 1946 that was denounced by Gandhi.

All states depend on armed bodies prepared to use violence against those their rulers' decree as enemies – external or internal. Sometimes the level of force is relatively small, as when police smash up a demonstration or a picket line. But faced with a serious threat such forces will use horrific violence even when their opponents insist on a commitment to peaceful methods as Chile in 1973 demonstrated. Any movement that stands for revolutionary social change but rules out the use of force when necessary condemns itself to destruction and its supporters to unnecessary suffering.

Monbiot's claim that there is no way to beat the violence of capitalism ignores the system's dependence on wider social processes. The position of any ruling class rests on its economic power and ideological dominance as well as its monopoly of physical force. Revolutionary situations arise when mass movements involving millions of people lead to the near paralysis of the state. They involve mass strikes, factory occupations, mutinies, the formation of workers' and soldiers' councils, huge demonstrations and deep splits in the ruling class. Revolution is possible at such points if the mass movement is prepared to use armed force to disarm those military and police units still committed to the old order.

Revolutionary ferment invariably has its effect on the rank and file of the armed forces. After all, they are people from working class or lower middle class backgrounds and have either been conscripted or joined because the military seems a secure job. They can hardly avoid being influenced by the insurgent mood affecting their brothers, sisters, parents and former school friends. But the strict discipline imposed by the officers and NCOs prevents them giving open expression to their feelings. Those that threaten to disobey orders can expect the harshest punishment – during normal times, long sentences in military prisons, during wars or states of siege the firing squad. So in Chile in 1973, naval NCOs who showed sympathy with the mass movement were thrown into prison and tortured. In Germany in 1917, when sailors organised a peaceful strike, the officers listened to their complaints, asked them to disperse and then organised a squad to arrest and execute those they considered the ring leaders.

Any successful revolution depends on the rank and file of the armed forces being prepared to use their arms to disarm their officers and dissolve the most reactionary military units. The key moment in the establishment of the Paris Commune in 1871 came when a group of working class women persuaded soldiers moving heavy guns to hand them over to the people. In Russia in February 1917 three days spent confronting mass demonstrations left many soldiers sympathetic to the rising and some of them took the initiative to arrest their own officers. In Barcelona in July 1936, when the generals initiated a coup to impose fascism across Spain, it was the resistance of poorly armed militias in Barcelona set up by anarchist union the CNT and the Marxist party, the POUM, that persuaded a section of the army, the Assault Guards, to join the resistance.

In each case, the initiative from workers outside the army was the key to giving the rank-and-file soldiers the confidence to take a stand against their reactionary officers. They would only take such a stand if they felt the workers movement was going to go all the way – not merely exert pressure on the army, but join with the soldiers to break the control of the officers and prevent punishment of the soldiers. That did not necessitate massive force. One hundred armed privates can confront one armed officer with minimal violence. But it does require a clear determination to use force if there is any resistance. Non-violence is not an option for soldiers intent on a successful mutiny, for it leaves the officers free to organise violent action against them.

When the most active sections of the masses and the minority among the rank-and-file of the armed forces are organised to act decisively the level of real violence – of deaths and injuries – is invariably small. By contrast, when the advanced sections are disorganised or pacifist feelings prevail the level of violence from the other side will be very great.

What is vital is the level of success in drawing the most militant sections of workers into a revolutionary organisation with wide influence not only in the workplaces and localities, but also in the armed forces. Only such an organisation can set out to coordinate the actions of those in the barracks who secretly sympathise with the revolutionary goals of the wider movement.

10:
Revolutions of
the 20th century

"ONE OF the world's most important and terrible events", was how a Radio Three announcer introduced an evening of programmes to mark the anniversary of the Russian Revolution. The centre-piece was a commentary by historian Orlando Figes, whose popular history of the revolution, *A People's Tragedy* (London, 1997), ascribes the events of October 1917 to Lenin's "bloodlust". To Figes, October 1917 and the horrors of Stalinism were one and the same thing.

This is a mantra opponents of revolution love to repeat: revolutions always lead to disaster, they say, and the only way to protect civilisation is to support the power of millionaires and multinationals or aristocrats and kings. To sustain this argument, they have to ignore the most elementary fact – that the basis of Stalin's power from 1929 until his death in 1953 was utterly different to that established in October 1917.

The revolutionary government of 1917 was based on elected delegates to a workers' council. It had the support of 67 per cent of the delegates elected in October 1917 and 74 per cent of those chosen in elections three months later. Such elections took place against a background of unfettered debate between newspapers and periodicals supporting different parties. Within the Bolshevik party, overwhelmingly made up of workers, there was free and open debate for at least the next four years.

The first years of the revolution were characterised by social transformation – the establishment of workers' control over the managers in the factories, the division of landlords' property among the peasants, the granting of self-determination to oppressed nationalities. A mass of social reforms, far in advance of those in any capitalist country at the time, gave women the vote in soviet elections, legalised divorce, established crèches, removed laws against homosexuality, ended discrimination against Jews and opened education to all.

By contrast, there were no workers' councils under Stalin. The supreme soviet of his 1936 constitution was a fake parliamentary structure, for which elections were not free. There was only one party, and all newspapers and periodicals slavishly followed its line. The majority of the party members were not workers, but managers, state bureaucrats and full-time party officials. No party member, high or low, was allowed to present any policy different to Stalin's. Anyone who tried was imprisoned and usually executed.

Stalin's party continued to call itself the Communist Party of the Soviet Union (Bolsheviks). But it had nothing in common with the party of 1917. Only 1.3 per cent of the 1.5 million members in 1939 had been members in 1917 and only one in 10 of the 200,000 surviving Bolshevik party members of 1918 were still in Stalin's party by then. Of the 15 members of the first revolutionary government, 10 were executed or murdered on Stalin's orders, four died naturally and only one – Stalin – survived. Hundreds of thousands of revolutionaries were killed by the secret police or died in labour camps. As Leon Trotsky put it before Stalin had him assassinated, there was "a river of blood" between Bolshevism and Stalinism.

Some people argue that because Stalinism arose in Russia after the revolution and involved some of those who played a part in the revolution, there must be a connection. But one event following another does not prove causation. A factory might make an object out of iron. If it is left in the rain and rusts until it is useless no-one in their right mind would argue the factory caused the rust. Similarly, one cannot simply say that a revolution is responsible for something that happens several years later. You have to look at the impact of other factors.

HOW THE REVOLUTION WAS STRANGLED

Karl Marx and Frederick Engels argued that a socialist society could only be built once advanced capitalism was established. Classes emerged in the past, they said, because natural scarcity prevented the putting aside of wealth to advance civilisation or improve production without one section of society exploiting the rest. Capitalist accumulation gave rise to such massive means of production it overcame that scarcity, but its class interests and structure prevented society moving forward. However, capitalism also made possible a revolution by the "overwhelming majority in the interest of the overwhelming majority".

Russia in 1917 was far from being an advanced capitalism. There were pockets of advanced industry in Petersburg, Moscow and a few other places, and it was the workers there who made the revolution. But four fifths of the population lived on the land, cultivating it under virtually medieval conditions, with minimal levels of literacy or knowledge of the world at large. For this reason, Lenin and other Bolshevik leaders argued until 1917 against any notion that a revolution in Russia could be a socialist revolution. They changed their minds because they saw what was happening as part of a revolutionary wave that could spread right across Europe – a process Leon Trotsky, who had come to this idea considerably earlier, called "permanent revolution". The advanced industry of Western Europe – especially of Germany – would provide the means to overcome the backwardness of Russia. If this did not happen, "we will perish", said Lenin.

It was not a crazy perspective. Not only Russia, but the other great empires that dominated most of Europe, Austria-Hungary, Germany and the Ottoman Empire, collapsed after 1917. At the end of 1918 there were workers' and soldiers' councils in Vienna and Berlin as well as Moscow and Leningrad. A workers' government controlled Hungary for several months. Italy went through "two red years" culminating in 1920 in the occupation of almost all the country's factories. A revolutionary movement erupted in Spain. In Britain, prime minister Lloyd George told trade union leaders they had the power to make a revolution if they wished.

Yet the attempt to spread revolution failed. Workers in the west were not immune to revolutionary ideas, but the leaders of the social democratic and Labour parties worked with the capitalists and the military to maintain the old order. "I hate revolution like the plague," said the German Social Democratic leader Ebert who became president in 1919. "Someone has to be the bloodhound," said his colleague Noske as he directed a mercenary army made up of officers from the old empire to crush strikes and uprisings.

The revolutionary regime in Russia was left devastated by three years of world war and was then invaded by 'White' armies run by the old ruling class. "The greater the terror, the greater our victories," declared the counter-revolutionary general, Kornilov, "We must save Russia, even if we have to set fire to half of it and shed the blood of three fourths of all Russians". "Anti-Semitic venom fairly dripped from the public pronouncements of Denikin's generals" a historian unsympathetic to the Bolsheviks records of the White armies: "As the pogroms of 1919 burst upon the Jews of the Ukraine with incredible ferocity, the enemies of Bolshevism committed some of the most brutal acts of persecution in the modern history of the Western world." Under the jurisdiction of General Kolchak "innocent men and women dangled by the scores from telegraph poles... and his men machine-gunned freight trains full of victims at execution fields along the railway".*

The devastation caused by the White armies was multiplied many times over by the intervention of all the major capitalist powers. Fourteen countries sent forces to try to crush the revolution, which seemed doomed to defeat in August 1919 as the White armies, backed by 200,000 western troops, advanced into the heart of Russia from three sides.

The revolutionary power survived, but at a terrible price. There were appalling food shortages and widespread cholera with reports of cannibalism in some parts of the country. Virtually all the factories shut down as raw materials ran out, until production was about one eighth of the pre-war figure. Half the workforce left the cities to find food in the countryside. The remaining half survived on meagre rations of bread obtained by armed detachments in the countryside. The working class that had made the revolution disintegrated, scattered across Russia. The revolutionary democracy that rested on this class inevitably suffered also. The militants were left in power with no mass base to debate the rights and wrongs of what they were

---

*   All quoted in W Bruce Lincoln, *Red Victory* (New York, 1989).

doing. But they knew that to abandon power would only bring the horror of the counter-revolution.

Victor Serge, an anarchist from Western Europe who went to Russia after the revolution, described the changes in the revolutionary power produced by foreign intervention and civil war. Up to June 1918, he wrote in his *The Year One of the Russian Revolution* (London, 1992):

The republic has a whole system of internal democracy. The dictatorship of the proletariat is not yet the dictatorship of a central committee or of certain individuals. Its mechanism is complex. Each soviet, each revolutionary committee, each committee of the Bolshevik Party or the Left Social Revolutionary Party holds a portion of it and operates it after its own fashion. All the decrees are debated during sessions [of the all-Russian Soviet executives] which are often of tremendous interest... Here the enemies of the regime enjoy free speech with more than parliamentary latitude...

But the pressure on the core area held by the revolution became almost overwhelming in June 1918. Not only were the White armies advancing, but the minority party in the revolutionary government, the Left Social Revolutionaries, assassinated the German ambassador in an effort to provoke renewed war with Germany and seize power themselves. Serge described how the pressure:

poses an unmistakable threat to the survival of the republic. The proletarian dictatorship is forced to throw off its democratic paraphernalia forthwith. Famine and local anarchy compel a rigorous concentration of powers in the hands of the appropriate commissariats... Conspiracy compels the introduction of a powerful apparatus of internal defence. Assassinations, peasant risings and mortal danger compel the use of terror... Soviet institutions... now function in a vacuum.

This transformation was not the result of some diabolical scheme of Lenin and the Bolsheviks as conservatives, liberals, social democrats and many anarchists have claimed since. It was the product of the strangulation of the revolution from outside.

THE STRANDED PARTY

The Bolshevik party itself underwent changes as it fought to keep the revolution alive. It began in 1918 as an overwhelmingly workers' party, with about 300,000 members – one in ten of those working in modern industrial plants. These were the activists who carried the burden of defending the revolution, forming the core of a Red Army involved in continual warfare, risking their lives to thwart counter-revolutionary conspiracies in the cities and desperately trying to keep industry running despite the absence of raw materials.

Most retained the socialist commitment that had held them firm during the years of repression and world war. But external pressures began to change the way many saw this commitment. People began to redefine the "dictatorship" required to secure the situation as no longer one exercised through democratic workers' organisation, but a dictatorship of the party.

At the same time, they were forced to rely on the assistance of large numbers of people from the middle and lower echelons of the old Tsarist administration, people with hardly an ounce of socialist spirit in them. Lenin was increasingly aware of the problems facing the revolutionary republic. In 1920 he argued: "Ours is... a workers' state with bureaucratic distortions." He described the state apparatus as "borrowed from Tsarism and hardly touched by the Soviet world... a bourgeois and Tsarist mechanism."

These pressures gave rise to a layer within the Bolshevik party and the state who were increasingly removed from the revolutionary democratic traditions of 1917. The person who came to express its attitudes was Josef Stalin, a second-level party figure in 1917 but increasingly taking the place of the dying Lenin by 1922. In his Testament, written in 1923 shortly before his death, Lenin called upon the party to remove Stalin from the post of general secretary. Such was the level of decay, even at the top of the party, that his advice was ignored.

Over the next decade, party members opposed to the Stalin group were driven out and a series of trials from 1936 onwards led to the execution of virtually the entire revolutionary generation of 1917. Leon Trotsky, universally recognised alongside Lenin in 1917-21 as the most important of the revolutionary leaders, was thrown out of the USSR and chased from country to country until his murder by one of Stalin's agents in Mexico in 1940.

None of this was an inevitable product of revolution. Rather, it was the product of the attacks launched against the revolution by the parasitic classes of the world. The Polish-German revolutionary Rosa Luxemburg, herself murdered in 1919 for trying to spread the revolution, recognised this as early as 1918. She wrote:

Everything that happens in Russia is comprehensible and represents an inevitable chain of causes and effects, the starting point and end term of which are: the failure of the German proletariat and the occupation of Russia by German imperialism. It would be demanding something superhuman from Lenin and his comrades if we should expect of them that under such circumstances they should conjure forth the finest democracy, the most exemplary dictatorship of the proletariat and a flourishing socialist economy... A model and faultless proletarian revolution in an isolated land, exhausted by world war, strangled by imperialism, betrayed by the international proletariat, would be a miracle [Rosa Luxemburg, *The Russian*

Revolution, available from www.marxists.org/archive/
luxemburg/1918/russian-revolution/ch08.htm].

A human being who is strangled ends as a smelly, dis-
coloured corpse crawling with worms, but no-one blames
the living person for that. The living revolution of 1917
was strangled, but no-one should blame that revolution
for the abomination it became.

STATE CAPITALISM

The murder of the revolutionary generation of 1917 was a
symptom of a fundamental change in Russian society. In
the 1920s, the Soviet Union was run by an increasingly
bureaucratised layer that still gave some indirect, though
increasingly faint, expression to the concerns of workers
and peasants. But in 1928 the problems of trying to
maintain an isolated state in a backward country in a capitalist world system came to head.

The bureaucrats around Stalin abandoned any real
hope of overcoming the pressure of the world system by
spreading revolution. They believed that left them only one
choice – to build up industry in competition with the rest of
the world by attacking the conditions of the peasants and
workers. They sent the army into the countryside to seize
first the crops from the peasantry, and then the land calling
this process "collectivisation". The regime did away with
the last elements of trade union independence and slashed
real wages by about 50 per cent. Oppression of national
minorities, who made up half the total population,
returned. Those who resisted the loss of their land or their
rights were sent to slave labour camps, where the number
of inmates grew from 30,000 in 1928 to 662,000 in 1930
and five million by the late 1930s. Intellectuals were bribed
or terrorised into submission, with the regime afraid lest a
poem or play should express the suffering of the masses.

There is a connection between the totalitarian structure that came to dominate the Soviet Union under Stalin and the policy of building industry in competition with the existing powers. But it is a connection that cannot be grasped by those who see Stalinism as a logical continuation of Bolshevism.

The industrialisation of economically backward countries has always been carried through at the expense of the mass of people, often by barbaric means. This was true of the industrial revolution in Britain, which depended on driving the peasantry from the land, putting children to work in factories, setting up workhouses to force people to take jobs, enslaving millions of Africans, and looting and impoverishing India. This process took 300 years. Stalin used similar means compressed into two decades – collectivisation of the peasantry, penal labour, slave camps, and the occupation of Eastern Europe after 1945. The barbarity was correspondingly concentrated.

Stalin called this system socialism and the party of the ruling class in Russia Communist. Most of the left in the rest of the world took him at his word, allowing right wingers to claim the Soviet Union proved socialism inevitably led to totalitarianism and hardship. Both sides missed the fundamental similarities between the Stalinist system and western capitalism – the subordination of the mass of people to a system of exploitation that allowed one set of rulers to compete economically and militarily with another.

OTHER REVOLUTIONS OF THE 20th CENTURY

The Russian Revolution was not the only upheaval of the 20th century. There were others in Mexico, Turkey, Germany, Austria, China, Egypt, Iraq, Iran, Vietnam, Cuba, Portugal and Nicaragua. But none of these involved workers organising democratically to establish their own power. Some of the revolutions involved mass movements that were held in check, overthrowing old monarchies to be replaced by the limited democracy permitted under capitalism. This is what happened in Germany and Austria at the end of the First World War, and in Italy at the end of the Second. In other cases, such as Mexico in 1920, a new bourgeois layer replaced an old one, using the slogans of revolution while conniving in the murder of revolutionary leaders.

There were other successful revolutionary movements that called themselves socialist or even Communist and Marxist. Yet examined closely, these were all a far cry from the revolutionary working-class democracy of Russia in 1917. They involved guerrilla armies of various sizes, run in an authoritarian manner, with many rank-and-file fighters from peasant backgrounds and leaders from the middle class. This was the character of the Chinese People's Army that swept into Beijing in 1949, of the Vietminh who defeated the French in Vietnam in 1954 and of its successor, the NLF, which drove the US out of South Vietnam in the war that ended in 1975. These forces embodied popular resistance to landlords and foreign rule. But they were never under democratic popular control.

The same was true of the regime of Abdul Nasser that took over in Egypt in the revolution of 1952, defying imperialism, redistributing land and nationalising 85 per cent of industry. It was true of the rebel army that took power in Cuba on New Year's Day in 1959. At no point were the mass of workers and peasants in Cuba involved in free debate about the direction the revolution should take or the aims of economic planning, and they enjoy no such involvement today. Cuban workers and labourers on the land can applaud measures they like and grumble quietly about those they do not. But they are not allowed to organise, to circulate publications with views different to those at the top, or to vote on proposals for the development of society.

Regimes such as Castro's in Cuba may have been better, at some point, than the society before – and Cuba deserves defending against strangulation by the US today. But this is not what revolution in the 21st century should be about. Indeed, all the regimes mentioned show signs of growing ever more like the western version of capitalism.

11:
Human nature and the alternative to capitalism

OPPONENTS OF revolutionary change always fall back on one key argument – human nature. They say this rules out any alternative to the competition and greed that characterise capitalism, that any revolution will simply give rise to new rulers who treat the mass of people in the same way as the old rulers. Revolutions inevitably "devour their own children", they say, quoting one of the moderates of the French Revolution, because of human nature.

These arguments draw on the notion of human beings as "naked apes", suggesting people have a tendency towards competitiveness and violence inherited from our primate ancestors. According to one writer:

Hierarchy is an institution among all social animals and the drive to dominate one's fellows an instinct three or four million years old... The human drive to acquire possessions is the simple expression of an animal instinct... The roots of nationalism are dug firmly in the social territory of almost every species of our related primate family... Our early human ancestors were engaged in continual bloody combat both with other species and with each other [Robert Ardrey, *African Genesis*, London, 1969].

Supposedly scientific disciplines, first socio-biology and more recently evolutionary psychology, have been used to give a sophisticated veneer to such claims. A book co-authored by one of the world's experts on insects, concluded there are genes for entrepreneurship, aggression, spite, conformity, xenophobia, gender roles and much more, and warned against conceiving of human nature "as relatively unstructured and largely or wholly the product of external socio-economic forces" (Charles J Lumsden and Edward O Wilson, *Genes, Mind and Culture*, Cambridge, Mass, 1981).

However, there is a key feature of the human genetic make-up which separates us from other creatures. Animals are genetically programmed in narrow ways that provide them with behaviour appropriate to a limited range of environments. We are characterised by immense flexibility in our behaviour that enables us to thrive in any part of the world. Our genetic speciality is that we are not specialised, not constrained by a range of instinctive behaviour. One result is that human beings can display very different forms of behaviour – ranging from great care for one another to selfishness and violence. The behaviour that predominates is not genetically determined.

For about 94 per cent of the time since modern human beings evolved our ancestors lived by foraging – what is often called hunting and gathering – before the development of agricultural and settled village life. Evolutionary biologists claim we were genetically determined during that period to behave as we do in present day society. But studies of hunter-gatherer societies report features very different to the stereotypical view of human nature. An early observer of the hunter-gathering Montagnais of Canada noted in 1834:

The two tyrants who provide hell and torture for many of our Europeans do not reign in their great forests – I mean ambition and avarice... not one of them has given himself to the devil to acquire wealth [Quoted in M Sahlins, *Stone Age Economics*, London, 1974].

More recently an anthropologist wrote:

There is no formal leadership, let alone class division, within these societies. Individual decision making is possible for both men and women with respect to their daily routines... Men and women alike are free to decide how they will spend each day: whether to go hunting or gathering, and with whom [E Friedl, *Women and Men: the Anthropologist's View*, New York, 1975].

Individual members of hunter-gatherer bands enjoy a level of autonomy infinitely greater than the mass of people in class societies. But it is not accompanied by selfishness.

The anthropologist Richard Lee, who carried out the most-thorough studies of one foraging society, the !Kung of South-West Africa, concluded:

It is the long experience of egalitarian sharing that has moulded our past. Despite our seeming adaptation to life in hierarchical societies, and despite the rather dismal track record of human rights in many parts of the world, there are signs that humankind retains a deep-rooted sense of egalitarianism, a deep-rooted commitment to the norm of reciprocity, a deep-rooted... sense of community [R Lee, "Reflections on Primitive Communism", in T Ingold and others, *Hunters and Gatherers*, vol I, New York, 1991].

Surprisingly, the most prominent right-wing economist of the 20th century, Friedrich von Hayek, shared the same opinion, although he did not like the fact, writing of dangerous "innate instincts" that led the mass of people to want "a just distribution, in which organised power is used to allocate to each what he deserves".

MANY HUMAN NATURES

None of this means there is a wonderful, benign human nature that automatically leads people to behave in positive ways. Rather, human behaviour is flexible and varies according to the situation in which people find themselves. The reason cooperation flowered in hunter-gatherer society was that humans had to cooperate and care for one another if they were to survive.

Humanity has lived in many different sorts of society since some of our ancestors began to adopt ways of living other than hunter-gathering about 10,000 ago – from light hoe agriculture, herding and fishing, to heavy plough agriculture, long-distance trading, handcraft production and finally, industrial production. There have been societies based on different kinship lineages, societies run by privileged religious or royal groups, societies dominated by warring groups of land owners and capitalist societies based on the exploitation of wage labour by rival owners of the means of production. Each society has given rise to characteristic forms of human behaviour that become so engrained in people's thinking that they appear natural. So in the Middle Ages, it was taken for granted across most of Europe, Asia and Africa that societies were formed of a fixed hierarchy of estates or castes into which people were born. Today, it is taken for granted that individuals compete with one another to improve their social position – despite the winners almost always being the children of those already at the top.

The transition from one such form of society – which we describe as feudal – to another, capitalism, involved a transformation in "human nature". The ways of thinking and acting today are specific to capitalist society, hammered into us by hundreds of years of this society.

This is not the end of the matter however; otherwise it would be difficult to see how we might build a society based on different values. Capitalism is based on the contradictory combination of what Marx identified as "social production and individual appropriation".

On the one hand there is a global productive system, drawing together the labour of billions of people, who work collectively in factories, mines, docks, warehouses, supermarkets, offices, farms – each connected by transport and communications networks to other units. This involves continual cooperative interaction between people. In every workplace people cooperate as well as compete. If they did not, the system could not function. Nurses do not look at time sheets or pay scales before dealing with a patient. Teachers do not demand a bonus before helping a child with reading difficulties. Soldiers often risk their lives for one another. These tendencies are increased by one of the many contradictions in the system – that as processes become more complex, control from above becomes more difficult. Management can never have anything like full knowledge of what is happening in a workplace and place ever greater reliance on elements of altruism and the desire to do a good job. Hence, the fashion for participatory schemes designed to make workers feel they have a real interest in their work. Even at the most mundane level, people are always getting help from others – whether asking for directions or requiring aid in an emergency.

On the other hand, all our efforts are framed by the relentless competition between companies and states that grab the fruit of our labour. The system breeds both cooperation and selfishness, altruism and aggression, care for others and hatred. The system distorts even our best intentions. To help their children, parents must compete for nursery and school places. Charities fighting poverty must battle other charities for money. It is these contradictions in "human nature" under capitalism that explain the mixture of hope and horror in recent history – the examples of selflessness and solidarity alongside atrocities and war.

The values of cooperation and mutual caring only really come into their own when those whose labour keeps the system going are driven to struggle against it. It is struggle that frees the cooperative spirit from the corrosive effects of competition. Even in small-scale, defensive battles people begin to embrace ideas that challenge the values of capitalism – notions of unity, solidarity and collective endeavour. Major battles lead to new ways of cooperating that point to a different way of running society. The cooperative spirit can find its highest expression in strike committees and picket lines, workers' councils and workers' militias.

Vast demonstrations produce a sense of solidarity that begins to dissolve the atomisation and selfishness of daily life. Great strikes allow people to develop this sense over days, weeks or months. But revolutions transform life totally. Hence, one of the extraordinary features of revolutions repeated in almost every account – crime declines even as police forces disintegrate.

In his *The Paris Commune of 1871* (London, 1937), Frank Jellinek wrote: "Public order had never been so little disturbed... Crimes of violence were few; robbery decreased notably." George Orwell described the mood in revolutionary Barcelona at the end of 1936:

Waiters and shop workers looked you in the eye and treated you as equals. Servile and even ceremonial forms of speech had temporarily disappeared...Above all there was a belief in the revolution and the future, a feeling of having suddenly emerged into an era of equality and freedom. Human beings were trying to behave as human beings and not as cogs in a capitalist machine.

In the Gdansk shipyard occupation of 1980, Polish film director Andzrej Wajda observed "an impression of calm, coolness, festivity, something lofty and extraordinary". By the end of that year, the workers' movement extended to every workplace in Poland, leading a sociologist to note: "Much of the interpersonal irritation and aggressiveness has disappeared. People are being nice to one another." A psychologist in Argentina reports how the development of a movement among the unemployed in 2001, the piqueteros, led to a rapid fall in psychological ailments.

In each case, struggle led to one element of "human nature" beginning to eclipse another. The social element in production, which unites people, escaped from the "individual appropriation" – the exploitation – which divides them. It is certain we will see a transformation of human nature in the revolutionary upheavals that are inevitable this century. What is not certain is whether these transformations become permanent or remain fleeting memories.

12:
Planning for human need

REVOLUTION IS about more than just overthrowing the ruling class. It is also about setting in train a new way of cooperating to make our livelihoods. This is necessary if humanity is to banish the material hardship that means one billion of the world's people go hungry each day, end the economic crises that periodically devastate the lives of millions more, end the colossal waste, environmental destruction and spending on weapons, and liberate the mass of the world's population from the daily treadmill.

Taking control of the means of production is the precondition for doing this. After all, few of the handful of people who control the multinational corporations and determine what happens to a huge chunk of the world's production have any particular skill when it comes to producing things. Their wealth enables them to pay other people to do what is required.

COMPLEXITY AND PLANNING

Those who support the present system tell us it simply is not possible to run things in any other way. The economist Alec Nove in his influential book *The Economics of Feasible Socialism* (London, 1983) argued modern production is too complex to be operated in any other way than through the market mechanisms of capitalism. It involves the production of too many different products, involving vast quantities of components. Any attempt to implement democratic planning would result in a bureaucracy of the sort that arose in the Soviet Union and be extremely inefficient. He argued: "The complex modern economy is unnameable to centralised direction" and "was bound to be overwhelmed by these tasks."

But if the technical complexity of production would be a problem for a democratically planned economy, it must also be problem in a world economy under the control of a few hundred billionaires. If these global production empires are to function profitably, they cannot assume the blind play of the market will provide the hundreds of thousands of components and other inputs they will need in three months or two years time. They have to try to plan to ensure they have these things.

This was true even 40 years ago. To produce a light car range the UK firm Rootes then had:

to order, correctly schedule and marshal no less than 16,000 different parts... to be fed through the production machine in such a way that thousands of variations can be made on a handful of basic models... the company was forced to work on an approximately five-year pattern on any given model [G Turner, *The Car Makers*, Harmondsworth, 1964].

The three supermarket chains that now dominate the sale of foodstuffs in Britain have to plan for a similar level of complexity. They want to guarantee the right mix of products in stores month after month, year after year. They are not prepared simply to hope that market forces will supply these. On the contrary, they have established a stranglehold over the food-processing industry, most of

British agriculture and many farmers in countries such as Spain and Kenya to ensure the output the supermarkets predict they will need.

However, capitalist planning is directed towards competition with rival firms, not the needs of the mass of people. It involves planning at the behest of those whose wealth gives them control of production – who have the power to manipulate market relations with small firms and farmers, and to redirect all know-how to their own purposes.

At the most basic level, if those running a multinational corporation can plan to achieve their ends, there is no intrinsic reason why democratic organs of workers' power could not do the same. Indeed, these would be better placed to do so, since the planning of each capitalist firm is continually undermined by attempts to damage the prospects of rivals. Plans are often abandoned half way through, creating chaos for other firms structured around supplying inputs. A workers' government that subjected all food outlets, for example, to democratically decided targets would not suffer from this. It would allow co-ordination across an entire industry instead of competition within it.

This does not mean someone trying to calculate in advance the number of various components to produce – any more than the individual corporations do this today. But it does mean decisions about the general direction of the economy being subject to democratic control. What matters is ensuring investment is directed to satisfying human need. Such democratic control should be exercised by elected and recallable representatives of those whose labour produces the wealth of society as a whole. They would decide whether to prioritise production of vehicles or of kidney machines, whether to shorten working time or use extra capacity to raise living standards.

The key decisions would have to be made centrally otherwise the big production units would be competing with each other to sell products. But once the major decisions are made in any economy, there would be an enormous leeway about how parts of the economy fit in to fulfil these. There is no requirement for centralised state control over every production unit. All that is needed is a basic democratic willingness by those running each unit – the workers who would take control of them in a revolutionary confrontation – to accept the need to find ways of fitting what they do to what has been decided in a free discussion.

This is the opposite of what happened under the so-called planning implemented by Stalinist, social democratic and third world regimes in the past. None of these submitted their plans to any organ of genuine democratic control. Those whose labour created the wealth in such societies were the last to have any say over what they produced and for what purpose. The competition between rulers – for example, between those in the Eastern bloc and those in the West, reflected in the arms race between the US and USSR – completely distorted their "planning", just as competition between one supermarket chain and another distorts the planning of both. It was not the complexity of the economies that created chaos, but the attempt to compete with the giants of world capitalism. The Soviet economy at its height was less than half the size of the US economy. The pressure of competition was correspondingly greater as a result, just as the corner shop has more difficulty competing with Tesco than does Sainsbury.

The revolution of the 21st century can open the way to genuine, democratic planning, by setting itself a very different goal to that of Stalin and his successors.

INTERNATIONALISM VERSUS
CAPITALIST 'DEVELOPMENT'

The revolution of the 21st century can only achieve its goals if it spreads from initial victories in one country to others. The history of attempts at "socialism in one country" shows this to be a blind alley. Capitalism, as an international system, has created an uneven distribution of resources globally and, along with that, an international division of labour. No one country contains the resources necessary to fully satisfy human needs.

This applies even more to individual third world countries. After centuries of pillaging by imperialism, many are too impoverished to find within their own borders the means to industrialise to the level of the existing advanced countries. Those third world countries that have developed have done so on the basis of vicious, dictatorial repression against the mass of workers and peasants: this was true not just in Russia and China, but also Taiwan and South Korea. Even in Cuba, which many people on the left see as a better example, the attempts at independent development in the 1960s collapsed after the failure to achieve the target of 10 million tonnes of sugar production in the 1970s, despite subordinating virtually the whole of economic life to this goal. This failure left Cuba as dependent on the Soviet Union as it had once been on the US and the collapse of the Soviet Union in 1991 left its people facing years of acute shortages and poverty.

What is needed in the 21st century is not development as it was seen by the middle classes of the third world and their multinational advisors in the 20th century – the attempt to squeeze out of the mass of workers and peasants the means to build up industry to a level comparable to that in the west. Rather, what is needed is a redirection of the huge resources that currently go to the local rich and the profiteers of the international system towards improving the lives of the mass of people. This would be a very different kind of development to that of the past. Ultimately, to achieve this depends upon gaining access to the resources not only of the poor parts of the world, but also to some at least of those controlled by capitalism in its heartlands.

But the mass of people in a single country do not simply have to sit back and wait for revolution elsewhere. They can make many immediate steps forward by taking power in their own hands. In conditions of acute economic crisis, the actual wealth produced in a country can be far below its potential level. In such circumstances a revolutionary transformation, involving the redistribution of wealth from the very rich to the mass of people can produce one-off improvements in living standards. It is absurd that in a country like Argentina, millions have gone hungry while vast amounts of food have been exported to pay interest on foreign debts and fatten the profits of the country's agrarian capitalists. But to sustain these improvements requires the creation of a new international division of labour, involving more than one country, something only possible by the spreading of the revolution.

There can never be a guarantee that a revolutionary breakthrough in one country will spread elsewhere. The Russian revolution of 1917 was, as we have seen, left isolated despite the wave of near revolutions in Germany and elsewhere in Europe. The Cuban revolution of 1959 created a tidal wave of hope elsewhere in Latin America, but this was not sufficient to wash away the local regimes which the US rushed to bolster up.

But such an outcome is not inevitable. Economic, social and political crises that open up the possibility of revolution are rarely confined to individual countries. The most important revolutionary upsurges in the last century all occurred on an international scale: 1917-20, 1934-36,

1943-45, 1956, 1968-75, 1989-91. In each of these, what happened in one country had a decisive effect elsewhere.

There are already signs of similar wave-like process at work in the first years of the 21st century. The antiwar protests on 15 February 2003 were not confined to individual countries but fed into each other drawing more of the planet's people on to the streets than any single issue ever before in human history. One estimate put the numbers marching around the world at 20 million. The movements in Latin America have strengthened each other, so that the continent is again alive to the hopes of revolution after two decades of defeat and demoralisation. In Europe, attempts by governments to push through neoliberal counter-reforms have created resistance across national frontiers, providing the impetus for the birth of a new left across the continent.

In either continent a successful revolution would have a very real prospect of spreading to neighbours, drawing into one democratically planned economic process the resources needed to offer people better lives in the long term as well as the short term.

Conclusion: Knocking on history's door

As I was writing the first draft of this book, the latest wave of revolt in Bolivia forced the Bolivian president Mesa from office. Emails, web pages and newspaper reports painted a picture like that of Petrograd in the summer of 1917, Berlin in January 1919 or Barcelona in the autumn of 1936. They described general strikes; columns of peasants marching on the city; the occupation of oil wells and airports; striking miners handing sticks of gelignite to striking teachers to throw against police lines; attempts to invade the presidential palace; threats by petrocapitalists in the east of the country to secede from the state; workers in La Paz chanting, "Civil War, Yes!"; the congress replacing the president while intimidated by huge, angry crowds. Yet they also finally described a truce between the two sides, with an end to the strikes and the departure of demonstrators from La Paz.

Karl Marx once wrote about the "mole of history", which bores away beneath the surface of events, suddenly revealing itself by undermining apparently all-powerful institutions. So it was in Bolivia.

The 1980s and 1990s had been terrible decades for the mass of the Bolivian people, just as they were in much of the rest of Latin America. Economic devastation was accompanied by neoliberal reforms resulting in living standards, already on a par with those in sub-Saharan Africa, sinking even lower. The working class was ravaged by closures, with the mass sacking of 20,000 tin miners (half the national total) in 1985. Politics became a game played between members of the white elite. The peasants, clinging to the plots of land given to them after a revolution in 1952, remained indifferent to calls for further struggle and the Bolivian left, once an important force, was a shadow of its former self.

Yet, barely noticeably, changes were slowly creating new forces able to challenge the established order. The peasantry began to find that its land was no longer secure, as agriculture became increasingly subject to market forces making it difficult for small farmers to hold on to what they had. The one crop with sure market potential, coca (from which cocaine is manufactured), was soon under threat from the US "war on drugs". The penetration of even the most remote villages by modern communications increased the consciousness of oppression among the indigenous two thirds of the country's population, the Aymara and Quechua peoples, whose first language is not Spanish. They began to organise against the inferior position imposed on them ever since the Spanish conquest of the Inca Empire 470 years ago, recalling with pride past risings in the eighteenth and nineteenth centuries.

Finally, the decline of other older industries was accompanied by the rise of a new working class. Indigenous people left the poverty of the countryside to find a livelihood in places like El Alto, the huge impoverished conurbation that hangs over the capital city, La Paz. So, while many commentators argued that Bolivia was undergoing "deindustrialisation" and that the country's working class was disappearing, the number of manufacturing workers actually rose – from 117,000 in the major cities in 1986 to 231,000 in 1995, with 38 per cent in workplaces of more than 30. These figures were matched by growing numbers of construction workers and miners of other metals than tin. By 1997, there were nearly as many wage earners – 1,400,000 – as there were peasants.

It was the logic of capitalism itself that gave active life to these new forces. The privatisation of water supplies in the Cochabamba region pushed up water prices for workers and peasants alike, causing tens of thousands to demonstrate, fight against the police and to discover in 2001 that by blocking roads they could bring the country as a whole to a halt. Success in beating privatisation in Cochabamba led to emulation of the tactics elsewhere, with protests and blockades by the coca growers and indigenous organisations. This example in turn created a new spirit of struggle in working class areas like El Alto and breathed life into the previously quiescent union federation, the COB, with the election of new leaders.

News that the government of the neoliberal president Lozada was selling off the country's one great prospect for wealth, its recently discovered gas reserves, to multinationals brought the ferment to a head in October 2003. What began as spasmodic agitation suddenly erupted into mass strikes and confrontations after the police shot down scores of protesters marching towards La Paz. It was then that El Alto became the centre of the movement. It was then too that miners rediscovered their old traditions and militancy by marching with gelignite in clenched fists to join the masses in the capital.

The October rising led Lozada to flee the country in a helicopter (the third Latin American president to do so in three years). But there was neither the consciousness nor the organisation among the hundreds of thousands of protesters in La Paz and El Alto to determine who replaced him. His deputy, Mesa, took his place in the presidential palace and the mass of demonstrators departed, believing they had won a great victory but neoliberal policies continued as before. The next day at an expanded meeting of the COB union, delegate after delegate lamented the fact that they had not been able to raise the idea of a workers and peasants government.

As is often the case in revolutionary upheavals, the first successful uprising was followed by a period of precarious stability. The new government made attempts to divert popular anger into nationalist agitation against Chile, which had annexed Bolivia's coastal region and blocked its access to the sea more than a century before. President Mesa held a referendum over the gas issue and managed to get away with phrasing the issue in such a way as to get a majority. Attempts at new mobilisations never seemed to get up a head of steam to repeat the October events.

An important factor in the impasse that followed October 2003 was the way, as also in past revolutionary upheavals, certain political figures and formations that had helped to lead the movement forward at previous stages now no longer did so. Indigenous leaders like Felipe Quispe of the Union of Peasant Workers had played an important role in articulating grievances against the Spanish speaking white elite who dominated official politics. But they allowed justified resentment at past treatment by the mestizo (mixed race Spanish speaking) section of the masses to divert them from pushing forward the struggle against the common enemy.

Evo Morales and his MAS party was the other channel for indigenous bitterness. They called for a constituent assembly to remould the country's political institutions to reflect its ethnic make up. But dazzled by the large vote for president that Morales received in 2002, they followed a strategy of keeping a weak Mesa in power so that Morales would eventually have the chance of succeeding him by constitutional means in 2007 and so they urged a "yes" vote in Mesa's gas referendum.

The COB union leaders took a more left wing stance, denouncing the gas referendum and urging people to abstain or spoil their ballot papers. But their traditions were still very much that of the old working class, and had little influence among the newly radicalised indigenous forces, treating as a diversion their demand to be part of a new democratic political structure. As a result, Mesa not only stayed in office for 21 months, but for most of that period enjoyed a degree of support among many of those who had taken to the streets in October 2003.

But things do not simply stand still when a mass movement gets stuck in an impasse. Those associated with the old order forget their fright and began to reassert their belief in their god-given right to rule. Mesa's government became increasingly like the overthrown Lozada government, preparing a law which left the majority of the gas and oil profits in private hands. Meanwhile in the lowland region in the east of the country around the city of Santa Cruz, where the gas and oil reserves are located, capitalist interests insisted that they would declare autonomy from the rest of the country if there was an attempt to use petroleum wealth for any purposes other than their own. They looked to support from the US and the supposedly left centre governments of Brazil and Argentina, whose oil companies are involved with Shell and BP in profiting from Bolivia's petroleum resources.

This was the spark which reignited the urban and rural masses in June 2005. They saw the one chance of using the country's wealth to overcome their poverty snatched away from them. They moved as they had 21 months previously to close down the whole country and besieged the presidential palace and congress.

The ruling class was paralysed. Mesa tried to hold on by balancing between the secessionists in Santa Cruz and the mass movement. He promised a constituent assembly to rewrite the constitution in a way that would please Morales and his supporters and a referendum on autonomy that would please the Santa Cruz petro-capitalists. Condoleezza Rice pledged her support for Mesa, and Morales opposed driving him from office. But the movement on the streets was more powerful and more radical than ever. The nationalist language opposing gas profits going to foreigners now became class demands for gas nationalisation in the interests of the workers, the peasants and the urban poor.

When it became clear Mesa was beyond saving, the Congress decamped to Sucre from La Paz in the hope of escaping the siege and resolving things according to the wishes of its neoliberal majority. They placed their hopes briefly in Mesa's constitutional successor, Vaca Diez, a representative of the Santa Cruz oligarchy. But it was already too late. They were besieged in Sucre too, as the workers movement paralysed all transport across the country. Congress passed over Vaca Diez to appoint as interim president Eduardo Rodriguez, head of the supreme court – but for six months only before elections.

Meanwhile, the hierarchy of the Catholic Church urged a "truce", warning of the dangers of "extremism", the Brazilian and Argentine governments applied pressure, and the US ambassador gave his seal of approval to the deal. After hectic negotiations, Evo Morales too backed it when he was assured there would be elections and the constituent assembly (a key factor in his decision, according to the reputable Buenos Aires paper *Clarin* was a cell phone call from Hugo Chavez advising him to do so). It was enough to signal the end of the demonstrations and a return to work by most of the strikers, tired after three weeks of struggle and suffering from food shortages as the road blockades stopped food arriving in the cities.

The Bolivian events illustrate all the points made in this book. The globalisation of capitalism tears people's lives apart, often demoralising them at first, but then pushing them into situations where they feel they have no choice but to fight back. Precisely because capitalism cannot manage without an exploited class, it creates a new working class with the power to fight just as it destroys much of the old working class. Bolivia also demonstrates how a successful struggle can suddenly inspire a score of others and as this happens apparently forgotten traditions of solidarity and insurgency are reborn. With this, people's attitudes to each other and to the state begin to be transformed, until they can conceive of a revolution taking place with the working class becoming the ruling class and the mass of people taking control of their own lives.

But Bolivia also shows how these things by themselves are not enough to bring about the change which people want. The movement paralysed the structures of power of existing society. But it never posed an alternative of its own. Without such an alternative, even feeding its own supporters was an insuperable problem. As the coordinating committee of the struggle in Cochabamba put it:

We have seen two things in the May-June struggle. On the one side, the magnificent force of the social movements is capable of paralysing the country and dealing with the manoeuvres of big business and the bad governments. On the other side, we have not been capable of imposing our own decisions and objectives on these same governments, although they are in the worst crisis they could face...

In the June crisis there was a moment when the whole question of who held power in society was in the balance. One can never be sure in such circumstances whether the workers and peasants movements could have taken power into their own hands. The solidity of discipline in the army and police in such a potentially revolutionary situation can only be tested in practice – you engage in battle and then you see. But on this occasion the decisive battle was not engaged.

There was a potentially revolutionary situation in Bolivia. The ruling class was divided. The working class, the peasantry, the urban poor, even the mass of self-employed street traders felt things could not continue as before. There were signs that sections of the army were wobbling. But two additional elements needed to turn the potential into reality did not exist – there was no workers' council or other popular form of revolutionary democracy that could unite the whole of the popular masses into a single organism standing in opposition to the old state. Nor did there exist an organised network of revolutionaries, a party, drawing together the most determined and militant activists in each of the various fronts of struggle that had emerged since the first victory in Cochabamba.

In the last days of the June struggle some activists did begin to look towards creating structures from below that could provide the first elements of democratic forms of self organisation. There was an initiative in El Alto for a Popular Revolutionary Assembly to take control of the city, to defend and feed it. In Cochabamba, the coordinating committee drew the conclusion that there had to be discussion about how to "little by little create forms of our own self government." But these initiatives came too late and with too little impetus to influence the outcome in June. People talked of an El Alto Commune but it never came into being.

The Bolivian struggle is far from over. The impact of the near-revolutionary events in June 2005 was to sweep Evo Morales to electoral office as president in December of that year on a programme of progressive reforms. But capitalism cannot satisfy the aroused hopes of the workers, peasants and indigenous peoples. Even the limited reform measures that have been implemented have roused the rich in Santa Cruz to build armed organisations that threaten to tear the country in two.

It remains to be seen what will happen next. But the real importance of the Bolivian events is not what they mean for one relatively small country. It is that they show how the endless uncertainty that characterises global capitalism repeatedly breeds potentially revolutionary resistance. The same spirit of resistance is to be seen in Venezuela. As in Bolivia, a government pledged to satisfy the needs of the mass of people still rules over a capitalist society, with massive concentrations of private wealth and enormous inequality. But also as in Bolivia, the surging desire for change from below, expressed in very large government demonstrations for "revolution" and "socialism of the 21st century", has created a rift between the classes. This will have to be resolved at some point in the future either by creation of a new state based on the democracy of workers and other exploited groups, or by the return of the old order.

Resistance is not confined to Bolivia and Venezuela, or even to Latin America. It is beginning make its mark on every continent. Things cannot be otherwise, since globalisation means global economic crisis, a global war drive, global environmental devastation and all the social convulsions that come in the train of such things. The rulers of Europe and North America tell workers they have no future unless they lower their wages, lengthen their working hours and worsen their conditions in order to compete with the workers of India and China. All this can only mean that there will be bitter class battles in the most advanced parts of the capitalist system as well as in the poorer parts.

None of this guarantees successful socialist revolution anywhere. Those who defend the existing system spend billions on arms; they have their police and their secret police, bribes for those who dance to their tune, a squalid gutter press, long experience of dividing and ruling and the ability to rely on habits of deference among those they oppress. Those who think nothing of blasting tens of thousands of people to death in order to establish their control over oil wells will do anything to try to stop a challenge to all their wealth and power. And yet they cannot break their dependence on us, the four or five billion people who labour for them in factories, fields, mines, offices, railway networks, truck depots, warehouses, power stations. Without our class they are nothing. And since their system cannot guarantee a fixed, stable existence for our class, revolts will flare up again and again in the present century as in the last. The question is not whether there will be revolutions in the century ahead, but in which direction those revolutions will go. Will they be snuffed out, as so often in the last century, as people put their trust in the lies and false promises of those who rule over them? Or will the new movement of the last few years rise to the task of uniting into revolutionary organisations all those among the exploited and oppressed able to see a little further than their fellows the evils of the system and the possibilities of overthrowing it.

Also by Chris Harman:

A People's History of the World

"I have had many people ask me if there is a book which does for world history what my book A People's History of the United States does for this country. I always respond that I know of only one book that accomplishes this extremely difficult task, and that is Chris Harman's A People's History of the World. It is an indispensable volume on my reference bookshelf"

Howard Zinn, leading US historian and radical

The Fire Last Time: 1968 And After

1968 was a watershed. Millions fought against war, exploitation and dictatorship. This fantastic history traces these great battles and examines the strengths and weaknesses of the radical movements that emerged in these years.

The Lost Revolution: Germany 1918 to 1923

A history of a great revolutionary upheaval, now almost forgotten. Chris Harman rescues it from oblivion and shows how close victory was, and why it ultimately eluded the revolutionaries.